The Butcher Baker

Life of Serial Killer Robert Christian Hansen

Jack Smith

MAPLEWOOD
– PUBLISHING –

Contents

A Hunter of Human Prey _____ 1

Honing the Hunter _____ 5

Criminal in the Cold _____ 9

The Prey Escapes _____ 15

Hunting the Hunter _____ 21

Psychological Analysis _____ 27

Those Who Fell Prey _____ 43

The Trial _____ 61

Caging the Hunter _____ 67

Modern Portrayals _____ 71

Further Readings _____ 77

Appendix: The Timeline _____ 79

Also by Jack Smith _____ 86

References _____ 89

A Hunter of Human Prey

"The best sport in the world," agreed Rainsford.
"For the hunter," amended Whitney. "Not for the jaguar."
"Don't talk rot, Whitney," said Rainsford. "You're a big-game hunter, not a philosopher. Who cares how a jaguar feels?"
"Perhaps the jaguar does," observed Whitney.
"Bah! They've no understanding."
"Even so, I rather think they understand one thing—fear. The fear of pain and the fear of death."
"Nonsense," laughed Rainsford. "This hot weather is making you soft, Whitney. Be a realist. The world is made up of two classes— the hunters and the huntees. Luckily, you and I are hunters. Do you think we've passed that island yet?"
"I can't tell in the dark. I hope so."
—"The Most Dangerous Game" by Richard Connell

Richard Connell wrote his famous short story "The Most Dangerous Game" (also known as "The Hounds of Zaroff") in the early 1920s. By the 1930s it was a movie. The story involved two big game hunters ending up stranded on an island where they intended to hunt jaguars. Instead, they become the prey as a man named Zaroff hunts them with his hounds. A perennial fixture on high school reading lists, the story would take on a macabre new popularity because of a man born over a decade after it was published. Beginning in the early 1970s, Robert Hansen would put his own spin on "The Most Dangerous Game." In his version, women would be sent into the Alaskan wilderness naked and blindfolded and then hunted down like animals.

1

Raised by strict, religiously overbearing parents, afflicted with a stutter and acne scars, Robert Hansen grew up to become a withdrawn loner. Slowly, a hatred for people, especially women, began to build. He began his life of crime by burning down a city garage used to house school buses. Moving on from there, he became a small-time thief and then discovered the world of prostitution. His anger, though, wasn't satisfied by paying for sex: He would hold working girls at gunpoint, handcuff them, and then rape them. And once he had the wilds of Alaska for his backyard, he turned to murder.

Nevertheless, Robert Hansen was regarded as a polite—if quiet—youth during the early years when he worked in his father's bakery. He ended up purchasing and running a bakery of his own in Alaska. He also became a skilled hunter who collected magnificent trophies of the state's big game. Anchorage residents had no idea what was hiding under the surface. Even after he was arrested, his standing in the community made rape victims reluctant to come forward. Many people just couldn't believe that the man they knew for his fresh donuts and hunting prowess had been killing more than just elk.

The unassuming loner blended in so well that local investigators ended up needing the help of the FBI Behavioral Analysis Unit and the expertise of criminal psychologist John Douglas. Douglas is well known for his book *Mindhunter* and his work on many high profile murder cases. He was able to complete a profile that matched Hansen perfectly, helping investigators sift through the false alibis behind the public persona to find the evil man hiding in plain sight.

Once the profile was complete, it wasn't hard to match it to Hansen. One of his victims, Cindy Paulson, had escaped his clutches only months before and had actually identified him as her rapist. However, Paulson was a prostitute, and Hansen was a respected member of the community, so in a "he said, she said" situation, his word had prevailed—with a little help from a seemingly convincing alibi. But when police got Douglas's profile, Hansen matched. With only the alibi to prevent the evidence from lining up perfectly, they took a harder look at it—and it wasn't long before that alibi fell apart and the truth came out.

Hansen had habitually targeted prostitutes and strippers. He'd gone as far as sending his family away on vacation so he could use his basement as a torture chamber where he held women handcuffed to a pole or hanging from a meat hook, biting, scratching, beating, and raping them. And then he got an airplane. His victims became prey, forced to run naked and afraid through the woods of Alaska as he hunted them down and shot them. Their bodies were buried in shallow graves or dumped along rivers. Hansen took a nightmarish tale and made it a real life scenario for his victims.

Understanding the psychology behind hunting and killing vulnerable people in this manner requires some insight into Hansen's history and how he grew up. Although the great debate of nurture versus nature is still going strong, it's fairly clear that what people live through as they're growing up—and how they adapt to it—has a reflection in their adult lives. Even with the best intentions, overbearing parents can cause an inward dip in a child's self-esteem and self-confidence. Hansen's parents went further than most, instilling a need for normalcy and perfection. They wanted a hard worker. They forced him to write with his right hand instead of his dominant left hand. They pushed him toward certain religious beliefs. Adding that to Hansen's acne issues and severe stuttering problem, he had a difficult time fitting in with kids his age. Puberty was a challenge, and girls weren't very kind. His anger turned inward and grew. Although there's no record of it, it seems entirely possible that he was killing animals and setting fires long before his teen years. And when he did get into hunting, an acceptable form of killing animals, he did so with a passion.

Robert Hansen, dubbed the "Butcher Baker," killed at least 19 women. Taking the crime escalator to the top, Hansen went from petty thief and arsonist to rapist to serial killer over his lifetime, all while maintaining the facade of a shy and gentle family man. He was a baker in Anchorage, Alaska, a husband, and the father to two children. But there are at least 30 women who lived through the horror of being kidnapped, raped, and abused by Hansen—and at least 19 who did not survive their encounters with the hunter at all.

Honing the Hunter

Robert Hansen's career as a baker started in his childhood. Christian Hansen was a Danish immigrant who had his own bakery with his wife, Edna, in Pocahontas, Iowa. On February 15, 1939, Edna gave birth to Robert Christian Hansen, their only child. Christian was a strict family man. He and Edna insisted that Robert work in the family bakery for the majority of the time that he wasn't in school. They also insisted that their left-handed child use his right hand as the dominant hand. Although there is no indication of actual abuse, his parents' controlling tendencies seem to have added a lot of stress to an already anxious child.

Hansen had issues with both a bad stutter and severe acne. He would tell interviewers that his face was "one big pimple" as a teenager and that the forced use of his right hand amplified his stuttering problem. Friends were few and far between, and none were very close to the skinny, shy, awkward child.

As Hansen got older, he experienced even more difficulty with children at school. He was often teased and picked on by the other students. His biggest problem was with the girls. The most attractive girls, to Hansen, were the meanest to him. It was at that time that a slow hatred for females began to bubble up inside of Hansen. The more abuse he received from his fellow classmates, the more withdrawn he became.

When he reached his teen years, Hansen began spending his scant free time out in the woods, hunting. He quickly became a rather adept hunter, and he found peace in the hobby. It was an escape from his life at home with strict, religious, overbearing parents, as well as the hardships he dealt with at school.

In high school, Hansen wasn't much for social activities. He had little money for such things and hardly any friends, and his parents were not fond of recreational events. Hansen did join a few school groups and sports teams so that he would be able to spend less time with his parents at the bakery and more time trying to socialize with students his age. He played basketball, ran track, sang in the school chorus, and was a member of the chess club. He took both driver's education and typing classes. Notwithstanding his attempts to fit in with his fellow classmates, he continued to be shy and withdrawn. His favorite activity was still hunting. Whether he was using a fishing rod, a bow and arrow, or a gun, Hansen preferred the solace of being out in the wilderness killing animals to interacting with other people.

In 1957, Hansen graduated high school and joined the United States Army Reserve. He trained at Fort Dix, New Jersey, and was then sent to Fort Knox, Kentucky. It was there, at age 18, that Hansen met with a prostitute and had his first sexual encounter. It wouldn't be the last, even for his short time at Fort Knox. In 1959, he went back to Iowa as an Army reservist. As a reservist, Hansen had to spend one weekend a month drilling; the remainder of the time, he worked in the family's bakery and volunteered at the Pocahontas County police academy as a drill instructor.

In between the Army, the bakery, and the police academy, Hansen met a local girl. They fell in love and were married in 1960. Six months later, Hansen committed his first crime. Hansen somehow induced a 16-year-old boy to help him set fire to the large Pocahontas County school bus garage. Later, Hansen claimed that he did it because he was angry at how the students and staff had treated him when he was in school. When the teenager went to the authorities and turned himself in, Hansen received a three-year sentence for the arson and his wife filed for divorce. He served 20 months of the sentence before being granted parole. During his incarceration, a psychological evaluation stated that he had an "infantile" personality. Hansen had just taken his first solid step into a lifetime of criminality.

Shortly after his release, Hansen met someone else. Within a short period of time, he was married to his second wife, Darla, who would remain with him until his arrest for murder. The couple moved to Anchorage, Alaska, during the oil boom of the early 1970s. Not only was it a chance for Hansen to start over with his new wife—it was also a place of great opportunity for an avid hunter.

Criminal in the Cold

Alaska not only had a booming economy, it also had a vast wilderness perfect for Hansen's favorite past time, hunting. It didn't take long for him to become proficient at hunting the wild game of the Alaskan forests and mountains. On four different occasions in 1969, 1970, and 1971, he had his trophy kills memorialized in the Pope & Young record books. Hansen's trophy room quickly became flush with monuments of his hunting exploits.

Eventually, though, hunting wild game ceased to satisfy him. Luckily for Hansen, the influx of people into Alaska had brought with it a fair amount of shadier activity. The majority of this activity was run by a Mafia boss from Seattle, Washington, named Frank Colacurio. The area he controlled was referred to as a "tenderloin"—the red light district of Anchorage. There were a multitude of strip clubs such as the Great Alaskan Bush Company, Arctic Fox, Wild Cherry, and Booby Trap. The unnamed dispensaries were the more abhorrent: brothels, magazine stands that sold child pornography and violent sexually explicit material, and drug dens. Crime in the tenderloin was high, featuring assault, robbery, prostitution, and even murder on a not infrequent basis.

Hansen got into the act with petty theft, then began perusing the ladies of the night. For 200 to 300 dollars, Hansen could get any one of these women into his vehicle. It didn't take long for him to move on to raping the women picked up. Most of them never reported the rapes; they did not believe they would be taken seriously, and at any rate it was something of an occupational hazard in their line of work. Even when the news broke years later about what Hansen had done to some of his victims, about the ones who didn't make it, very few of the survivors came forward. An unknown number could not come forward, as they had disappeared from the streets never to be seen again.

Prostitution is illegal in most of the United States for a few reasons. The first is to help prevent the spread of sexually transmitted and drug related diseases. The second is the lack of laws that would enable prostitution to be regulated as a legitimate occupation. Thirdly, prostitution is often associated with other criminal activity; where there is prostitution there are also drugs and often other forms of crime. Of course, the illegal nature of their profession and their proximity to other criminal elements makes prostitutes easy prey. Controllable by drugs and money, disposable in the eyes of sociopaths and solid citizens alike, they are often the target of rape, theft, abuse, and murder.

Many of Hansen's victims who weren't prostitutes were exotic dancers. In 1970s Anchorage, dancing in strip clubs was often a supplementary job for women who were trying to raise children, finish school, or just make enough to get by. In a place with long nights and a burgeoning population of unattached men seeking entertainment, exotic dancing was seen as a decent source of income, without the risk of working the streets or the requirement of sexual interaction. Some strippers also worked as call girls, but the majority did not. For Hansen, however, there was no difference. The strip clubs were mostly in the seedy, shady tenderloin district where reliable witnesses were few and far between. Exotic dancers therefore made easy targets, because it would be very difficult for them to prove that an assault had occurred—or even to get the police to take the complaint seriously. Many of those who disappeared forever did have missing persons reports filed by friends or relatives, but these were not usually a priority for authorities. The high-risk lifestyle was considered a person risk, and police tended to focus on the fact that these women worked in a field that catered to the criminal populace. This fact certainly allowed Hansen to get away with his crimes for longer than he would otherwise have been able.

In November of 1971, a woman pulled up to a stoplight in the Alaskan town of Spenard. She looked over to see Hansen and gave him a polite smile. Hansen lifted a gun and pointed it at her, demanding that she get out of her car and into his. She wisely drove away, and Hansen was arrested. While out on bail prior to the trial, he was arrested again, this time for the kidnapping, rape, and armed assault of an 18-year-old prostitute. Unfortunately for Hansen's future victims, the prostitute failed to show up in court on the day of the trial, and Superior Court Judge James Fitzgerald was forced to drop the charges in that case.

However, Judge Fitzgerald still wanted to keep Hansen off the streets, and he still had the charge of assault with a deadly weapon from the first incident. He later said that he recognized the type of man Hansen was and knew he was a probable repeat offender. The best he could do was to try to slow Hansen down. Unfortunately, he wasn't able to slow him down much. Sentenced to five years, Hansen was jailed in March and paroled in June, when he was moved to a halfway house under psychiatric supervision until November. In Hansen's eventual confession, he told police was already prowling around the red light district searching for his next victim the night he was released. He was the subject of more complaints in 1975, but one by one, the prostitutes dropped the charges. They were afraid that Hansen would go free and follow through on his threats to kill them if they told anyone.

Two women were already missing when Hansen was arrested again in 1977. 17-year-old Megan Emerick had gone missing on July 7, 1973, from Anchorage. Two years later, Mary K. Thill, a 23-year-old housewife, had gone missing from Seward. Hansen was not arrested for these disappearances, however; he had stolen a chainsaw. He was sentenced to another five years in prison. After a psychiatric evaluation, Hansen was diagnosed with behavioral and personality issues, including bipolar disorder. It was ordered that he follow a lithium-based treatment program, but this was never enforced. After one year in jail, Hansen was released back onto the streets.

He quickly resumed his hobby of kidnapping women off those same streets. To make his home available for this dark pastime, he sent his wife and children away for a vacation. Some of the women were raped and released; some went missing. In 1980, Hansen killed a dog belonging to one of his murder victims. He later told investigators that he was afraid that the dog would lead someone to her body.

In that same year, a body was discovered near Eklutna Road. The woman would be dubbed "Eklutna Annie," and is still unidentified to this day. In June, Roxanne Easland, a 24-year-old prostitute, went missing from Anchorage. Joanne Messina's body was discovered in a gravel pit after she disappeared from Seward in July. 41-year-old Lisa Futrell was last seen in Anchorage in September of 1980.

To society, though, Hansen seemed to be doing well. In 1981, Hansen claimed his house had been burglarized and his hunting trophies stolen, resulting in a settlement from his insurance company. He used the money to open a bakery in Anchorage. The insurance company, however, filed a fraud case when it was discovered that the missing trophies were still in Hansen's possession. His excuse was that he had found them in his yard and forgotten to report the fact to the insurance company.

In 1981, two more women went missing from Anchorage: 22-year-old Andrea Altiery and 23-year-old Sherry Morrow. The next year, Hansen bought an airplane, despite his lack of a pilot's license. The Piper Super Cub N3089Z became the key component of his hunting expeditions. Previously, Hansen had picked his victims up and handcuffed them in his vehicle before taking them to nearby rural areas. He now began to fly them out to the Knik River, where he had located a remote sandbar. It was there that he would begin his hunt. The women were stripped, raped, blindfolded, and then released. Hansen would hunt them with his favorite rifle before burying or dumping their bodies and then flying back to Merrill Field, where he kept his plane.

23-year-old Sue Luna was last seen in Anchorage in May of 1982. In September of 1982, the body of Sherry Morrow was found by the Knik River by an off-duty policeman who was out hunting. Paula Goulding, a 31-year-old stripper, went missing in April of 1983. Even as more women began to disappear and bodies began to pile up, Hansen was still maintaining his facade as a baker—and still randomly raping women he picked up in Anchorage's tenderloin district. And then, one of his victims escaped.

The Prey Escapes

Cindy Paulson was a 17-year-old girl who had fallen on hard times. She led a high-risk life working the streets as a prostitute in Anchorage. She had already seen the darker side of human nature up close and personal. And then one day a man picked her up and changed her life forever. It was the worst day of her life—and it was almost the last. She would be one of the lucky ones who survived, but only due to her strength and tenacity.

A sedan stopped to pick up Cindy Paulson on June 13, 1983. Cindy watched the man as they spoke. He was well dressed, but seemed a bit odd, quiet and nervous. Still, there was nothing to indicate that he had any violent tendencies. They discussed what he was looking for and the cost, and he agreed to pay Cindy $200 to perform oral sex. Cindy got into the car.

As soon as she was sitting in the seat, the man changed completely. He pulled out a gun and pointed it at her as he handcuffed her, threatening to kill her if she tried to escape or call any attention to them. He then drove them to his home, where he took Cindy down into the basement. She was forced to strip. He told her that no one would believe her if she tried to escape. He bragged that he was an upstanding citizen whereas cops would see her only as a prostitute and a liar. He also told her he had an alibi already in place. Cindy was already beginning to realize she might not survive the encounter.

Cindy was then tortured and raped repeatedly for hours. Her captor bit her nipples, sexually assaulted her, and then began to use tools, such as a hammer, to rape her. Eventually, he became tired and handcuffed her and chained her neck to a concrete support in the basement. Then he lay down on a nearby couch to take a nap.

When he woke up, he forced Cindy to dress hastily and return to the car. She had to crouch in the back seat as he drove, telling her that he was going to take her to his cabin. Cindy took her shoes and tucked them down into the rear floorboard of the back seat. She would later tell interviewers that she didn't think she would survive the encounter, so she wanted to leave as much evidence as possible to make sure the man wouldn't get away with it.

They arrived at a small airfield. Cindy began scoping out her escape route as he started moving items over to a plane. He uncuffed her and escorted her to the small aircraft, making her climb inside. However, he didn't secure her as he continued loading guns and supplies into the plane. Cindy saw her chance and took it. She took off, running toward the distant road, 6th Avenue. The man pursued her at first, yelling that he was going to catch her and kill her, but stopped when he saw a truck coming down the road.

36-year-old truck driver Robert Yount saw Cindy, handcuffs dangling from her arm and looking a little worse for wear, and stopped. She climbed in and he took her to the nearby Mush Inn to use a phone. She was trying to call her boyfriend at the Big Timber Motel as Yount left. As he got back on the road, he called the police on his CB radio to report that he had picked up a battered looking woman with no shoes taken her to the Mush Inn. Officer Greg Baker of the Anchorage Police Department went to the Mush Inn, but Cindy was no longer there. The receptionist told him that she had mentioned something about the Big Timber Motel. When he arrived there, Officer Baker found her in Room 110. She was sitting alone, still wearing the handcuffs.

As Officer Baker removed her handcuffs, she told him what had happened to her. She described the kidnapping, the torture she had experienced in the basement of a nice house in a decent suburb, and her abductor's plans to take her to a cabin they could only get to by plane.

The police were incredulous. Some instantly dismissed her story as unbelievable. Others were simply too familiar with the crime in Anchorage, and the criminals. To them, prostitutes were part of the problem. On the other hand, her description of the events and locations was clear and certain, and it was evident that she had suffered some kind of trauma. Officer Baker saw a terrified and beaten woman who was determined to make sure the man who had done this to her would not get away. For this policeman, the crime was too bizarre—and at the same time too strangely familiar—for him to let go.

At the police station, Cindy Paulson filed a formal report, writing down every detail she could remember. The suspect was described as a man in his 40s with reddish hair. Cindy told them about the sedan, the color and style, and that her shoes were in the back seat floorboard. She knew that the house had been in Muldoon. The plane was at Merrill Field, where the trucker had picked her up. After filing her statement, police took her back out to the airfield to see if she could identify the plane the suspect had put her in. Cindy pointed out the blue-and-white Piper Super Cub with the registration identifier N3089Z. She was then taken to the hospital for a physical exam and rape kit. It was confirmed that she had bruising and tearing consistent with sexual assault.

It was easy for police to trace the plane to Hansen. They went to his house and confronted him with Cindy's accusations. Hansen acted surprised and baffled, but readily agreed to cooperate and went down to the police station to make his statement. He was interviewed by an officer from the Anchorage Police Department's Sex Crimes Division, William Dennis. He claimed he had never seen Cindy, and even asked detectives, "You can't rape a prostitute, can you?" He admitted that his family was out of town on a European vacation, but said that his neighbors would give him an alibi—which did check out. His demeanor was calm and confident; in fact, the only suspicious aspect was that he was being accused of very serious crimes and yet was very composed and relaxed. He gave his permission for police to search his house and vehicle.

Investigators did a cursory search of the various locations tied to the alleged crimes. Cindy's descriptions of the interior of the home, car, and plane, as well as her shoes in the car, proved that she had been to all three places at some point. Since Hansen's statement suggested that Cindy was trying to extort him, police began to wonder if he had utilized her services but failed to pay her. Perhaps she was recalling details from that event and applying them to her accusations?

Hansen was known as a meek man and the owner of a well-loved bakery; Cindy was a teenage whore. Cindy had also refused to take a lie detector test. Hansen relied heavily on those facts to help him get out from under police scrutiny, and it worked. After checking Hansen's alibi with his friends John Henning and John Sumrall, Officer Dennis closed the case. Only Officer Greg Baker, the one who'd originally found Cindy at the Big Timber Motel, was still convinced that Hansen was getting away with a crime.

At the time, Anchorage had more than its share of crime—not to mention the increasingly obvious possibility that they had a serial killer on their hands. But police weren't focused on Hansen as being the potential perpetrator. To them, Hansen just didn't seem like the serial killer type. And despite Cindy's statements, her obvious knowledge of Hansen, his home, his vehicle, and his plane, the rape of a prostitute didn't rank high on their list of priorities. Only two members of the Anchorage PD weren't so certain: Officer Baker, and Detective Glenn Flothe, who had been working on the case of the murdered women popping up in the Alaskan wilderness.

18

Soon, the police would have another name to add to their growing list of potential serial killer victims. On September 9, 1983, the decomposing body of 31-year-old Paula Goulding was found along the banks of the Knik River. Paula had been reported missing over five months before, in April. She had been shot, the same as the others. A .223 caliber bullet was recovered. Most tellingly, Paula's body was found in the same spot that Sherry Morrow's had been almost exactly a year before (minus ten days). With this find, the local police decided that they needed help catching their serial killer. They called in the Federal Bureau of Investigation.

Hunting the Hunter

Alaska had dealt with another serial killer a decade before. Unfortunately, that killer was not discovered until after five women were dead. Aware that the law was closing in, he was on the run before the cops had even finished figuring out who he was. He fled on a motorcycle and ended up killing himself in a high speed accident. The Anchorage Police Department and the Alaska State Troopers were determined not to have a repeat, but the body count was rising and they still had no idea who their killer was. Detective Flothe called the FBI about his three confirmed victims of a possible serial killer. The FBI assigned the case to Special Agent Roy Hazlewood and criminal psychologist John Douglas.

John Douglas has since become a renowned criminologist. To the general public, he is best known for his 1995 book *Mindhunter*, which describes his work on the Hansen case. Douglas joined the FBI in 1970 after service in the Air Force. In 1976, he moved to the Behavioral Analysis Unit. Together with Robert Ressler, he pioneered the investigative techniques that gave rise to the television term "profiling." Douglas helped solve the 1979-1981 Atlanta Murders when he created a profile that matched the killer Wayne Williams. In both the West Memphis Three and Jon Benet Ramsey cases, Douglas told authorities they had their suspects completely wrong. Jack Crawford in Thomas Harris's *Silence of the Lambs* and Jason Gideon in the television series *Criminal Minds* were both based on John Douglas and the cases he was involved in. Douglas has written 13 nonfiction books and two novels. But what is a criminal psychologist, and is it the same as a profiler?

To understand how important John Douglas's expertise has been to certain cases, including Hansen's, you must understand what a "profiler" is and what it means. In the investigative world, the title "profiler" is not used. Criminal psychologists, behavioral scientists, criminologists, and forensic psychologists are specialists associated with what is referred to as profiling. Much like the fictional Sherlock Holmes, they look at all the clues and evidence, and using deductive reasoning and observation based on probability, they come to a conclusion as to how a crime was committed and who committed it. Everything from weapon to location to victim selection supplies a vast amount of information to a criminal psychologist. The manner in which the crime is carried out, what is and isn't left behind—every detail tells the investigators a bit more about the suspect.

John Douglas's criminal profile for the suspect in the Alaskan murders was very apt. Douglas stated that he was someone who was very insecure. He would have to be normal enough for women to not fear him at first, to go with him. He might have a lisp or stutter and maybe pockmarks or other facial deformities, something that made him self-conscious about his interactions with other people. He would be a loner, someone who normally would not fit into society, but he would have an occupation or position that would help him fit in regardless. He might even have a family. Based on the evidence of charring near some of the bodies, he would have a history of arson. Douglas said the killer was probably a hunter. The victims were all shot with a rifle—the same rifle—and found in the wilderness. Because of his hunting prowess, the murderer would have a trophy room or somewhere else to display his hunting trophies. With that idea in mind, Douglas predicted that his trophy collection would also extend to his victims. Once police got a search warrant, they would be able to find personal belongings of the victims in the killer's house. He would also have more minor crimes on his record, something that started prior to him working up to becoming a killer. The abuse of the victims showed anger and a desire for revenge against women, especially those who worked in the sex industry.

From *Mindhunter: Inside the FBI's Elite Serial Killer Crime Unit*, by John Douglas:

Hansen, I was surmising, regarded prostitutes in much the same way. They were people he could regard as lower and more worthless than himself. And he wouldn't need the gift of gab to get one to come with him. He would pick her up, make her his prisoner, fly her out into the wilderness, strip her naked, let her loose, then hunt her down with a gun or knife.

His MO wouldn't have started this way. He would have started simply by killing the early ones, then using the plane to fly their bodies far away. These were crimes of anger. He would have gotten off on having his victims beg for their lives. Being a hunter, at a certain point it would have occurred to him that he could combine these various activities by flying them out into the wilderness alive, then hunting them down for sport and further sexual gratification. This would have been the ultimate control. And it would have become addictive. He would want to do it again and again.

And this led me to the details of the search warrant. What they wanted from Jim and me was an affidavit they could take to court explaining what profiling was all about, what we would expect to find in the search, and our rationale for being able to say so.

Unlike a common criminal or someone whose gun is an interchangeable tool, Hansen's hunting rifle would be important to him. Therefore, I predicted the rifle would be somewhere in his house, though not in open view. It would be in a crawl space, behind paneling or a false wall, hidden in the attic: someplace like that.

I also predicted our guy would be a "saver," though not entirely for the normal reasons. A lot of sexual killers take souvenirs from their victims and give them to the women in their lives as a sign of dominance and a way of being able to relive the experience. But Hansen couldn't very well put a woman's head on the wall the way

*he would a big-game animal's, so I thought it likely he would take
some other kind of trophy. Since there was no evidence of human
mutilation on the bodies, I expected him to have taken jewelry,
which he would have given to his wife or daughter, making up a
story about where the piece came from. He didn't to appear to have
kept the victims' underwear or any other item we could account for,
but he might have kept small photographs or something else from a
wallet. And from my experience with this type of personality, I
thought we might find a journal or list documenting his exploits.*

When investigators applied John Douglas's profile to their possible
suspects, one man matched all of the criteria. Hansen had
pockmarks from severe acne, as well as a stutter. He worked in a
bakery. He wasn't well-known, per se, but people in the community
were aware of him and he seemed like a "nice, quiet guy" with no
outlandish behaviors. He was also an avid hunter; several of the
trophies in his trophy room were even in record books. He had a
history of arson, having burned down the bus garage back in Iowa.
Hansen also matched the physical description, and his vehicles
matched witness descriptions, from several Anchorage rape cases.
The icing on the cake was the witness statement of Cindy Paulson,
the one who got away. The only problem was that Hansen had an
alibi.

Police went back to John Henning and John Sumrall, the neighbors
who'd provided that alibi, and informed them that it was a crime to
obstruct a federal investigation. The friends had initially assumed
that Hansen's need for an alibi had something to do with his
insurance fraud case, but now they realized that he was being
investigated for more serious crimes. They quickly agreed to recant
their statements and admit that Hansen had not been with them
during the time that Cindy Paulson said the rape had occurred.

There were still issues with the District Attorney's office and the
Anchorage Police Department. Both were hesitant to focus on
Hansen as the culprit for the murders. Part of this was because he
had been arrested once, for the chainsaw theft, and had been

accused of a rape fitting the modus operandi of their serial killer and yet had been set free. If Hansen was the man, they had had the killer in their grasp and then let him go, and that was a difficult pill to swallow. Once the media realized that the authorities had failed to stop Hansen on at least two occasions, they would be in a lot of trouble with the community.

Detective Flothe, though, had been digging deeply into Hansen's past. He was still convinced that Cindy was telling the truth. Among his findings were the arrest for pulling the gun on a woman in traffic and the dropped charges of rape in the early 1970s. With this information, the vanished alibi, and John Douglas's profile, the evidence became too overwhelming to ignore, and the DA's office finally signed off on the warrant.

On October 2, 1983, Anchorage detectives followed Hansen to work. They told him he needed to come down to the station for questioning, and Hansen obeyed without a fuss. While he was being interviewed, two groups of investigators were sent out with warrants, one for his plane and one for his house.

The house was searched from top to bottom. Many weapons were found, most of them typical hunting guns and bows. At first, police were unable to find anything linked to the evidence recovered from the victims' bodies. Then one eagle-eyed officer found a secret wall space in the attic. Inside was a Remington rifle, pieces of jewelry from the victims' bodies, clipped articles from newspapers, a Winchester shotgun, a small single-shot pistol, several driver's licenses and other IDs belonging to the victims, and a .223 Ruger Mini-14 rifle. There was also a map behind his headboard—an aviation map with several red X's marked in the Alaskan wilderness.

Back at the police station, they were finally able to arrest their serial killer. Hansen was charged with insurance fraud, weapons violations, theft, kidnapping, and assault and his bail was set for $500,000. He became increasingly enraged as the charges were announced and the evidence from his home was laid out in front of him. Hansen requested his lawyers, and when they came, police could hear him screaming at them through the walls.

Psychological Analysis

In nature, there is a hierarchy of animal species based upon the predator/prey dynamic. Humans are now at the top of that list, as all of our former predators have become our easy prey thanks to modern firearms. Without a gun, what is a man to a full-grown bear, the man's fingers to the bears claws? With a gun, man is, uniquely in the animal kingdom, every animal's predator.

Animals in the wild hunt for food and to protect themselves by thinning overpopulated areas and removing threats to themselves or their pack. Many people still hunt for food, but many others hunt only for sport. And then there are those who hunt people, to deal with psychological issues or to feed some dark, internal need. Hansen hunted game for sport; he hunted people to satisfy his anger at himself and the people on whom he projected his psychological insecurities.

It seems baffling that someone could look at another person the same way he would look at a wild animal. How does a person hunt another person with no thoughts or feelings about what he is doing? The dark truth is that it is still in our nature, deep and primal, to hunt and kill. It is a part of us that has little to no use nowadays. For the most part, we have learned to deal with those urges, have moved far past those primal feelings and no longer feel the call of killing. Why should we? We don't have to fight for our homes, our food, our mates; we only fight over territory at a national level. There is no need for violence against others. Some, though, cannot dampen those urges.

There is also the fact that people like Hansen don't see other people as belonging to the same species. Such a man craves dominance and control. He doesn't feel for his victims, he doesn't see their tears or fear, and he has no thought that they are beings like him. To him, they are merely disposable things. They are animals to hunt and do with as he pleases. For a man like Hansen, the only thing that would improve hunting humans would be the ability to display his trophies and show the world how strong and powerful he is.

Nature versus nurture is an ongoing debate, but one that is increasingly viewed as incorrect. Current psychological analysis holds that *both* nature and nurture make people who they are. Two people who have lived through a similar situation may deal with the subsequent issues and problems differently based on how they process the experience and how their emotions react. This is explained in the article "Serial Killers: Nature vs. Nurture" on the website of the National Center for Crisis Management American Academy of Experts in Traumatic Stress:

Modern geneticists have pointed out that a nature-nurture dichotomy is clearly untenable, incorrect, and meaningless. The subject has to be discussed in terms of the continuous and complex interactions between an organism and its environment, and the relevant contributions of both sets of variables in determining the behavior of the organism (Athens 12)…

Sociologist Arnold Arluke compared the criminal records of one hundred and fifty three animal abusers with one hundred and fifty three non animal abusers and what he found in his study is that those who were animal abusers were five times more likely to commit acts of violence such as assault, rape, and murder against others. What was understood from this study is that serial killers in their childhood would resort to killing animals because they felt powerless against their parents who had control over them. Since these children did not have control in the household, they resorted to killing small animals in which they could exert their dominance and power over to do anything that pleased them (Fox 113).

In a study of sixty two male serial killers, Eric Hicky a criminologist found that, forty eight percent of them had been rejected as children by a parent or some other important person in their lives (Fox 113). Though this happens to many children, it certainly represents a turning point for those who become serial killers. Once rejected many of these killers begin to dive into their self-indulgences and are unable to understand how and who they are when going through puberty. "The social experiences which make people dangerous violent criminals are the significant experiences rather than the trivial ones in their lives (Athens 19).

That the truth lies on both sides of the age-old argument has been proven time and time again. Environment can most definitely have a bearing on how a person progresses from a given experience, but one's chemical make-up and physiology is an equally determinative factor. There have been many studies on the brains of killers, covering emotional impulse murderers, spree killers, mass murderers, and serial killers. With the exception of emotional impulse killers (those who murder in the heat of passion, whether anger or fear or some other reactive emotion), between 85-97 percent were deemed likely to have some kind of chemical imbalance or physiological brain defect.

How does this information pertain to Hansen's case? Hansen's parents were strict, religiously overbearing, controlling, and hard on Hansen. However, they were not particularly abusive, and they weren't neglectful. There have been serial killers with both better and worse childhoods, and yet all of them ended up killing. Hansen was not allowed to embrace who he was. He was a lefty forced to use his right hand. He loved sports and athletics, but his parents forced him to focus on family and the family business. Hansen had facial deformities in the form of severe acne and cysts that caused scarring by his late teen years. He wore horn-rimmed glasses, was tall and thin, and wasn't particularly handsome. His parents made him feel embarrassed about the ways in which he was different from others. The strict atmosphere and hard work under his father's thumb caused him to turn inward. His self-confidence and self-esteem dwindled, causing him to be shy and withdrawn.

These reactions, though, were not what made him a killer. They were merely stepping stones that allowed the chemical imbalances from which Hansen suffered to play a larger role in who he was. His parents were not at fault for what he became; they had no way of knowing that their strict upbringing would cause such an explosive reaction. It was merely the beginning. As Hansen grew up and had more interactions with society, his psyche was damaged. Pretty girls made fun of him when he was hitting puberty; just as he began to feel sexual needs, he faced sexual denial and repression. He didn't fit in.

Victims of abuse and rejection, serial killers find comfort in their fantasies and dreams that take them into a realm that only they can control. Psychokillers take their fantasies and make them a reality living their dreams. ("Serial Killers: Nature vs. Nurture")

This caused him to seek other ways to express himself and find a feeling of control over his life. Hunting became that outlet. With hunting, he was the boss. He had control. He decided what lived or died, and he became very good at killing. But using something as primal as death and killing as an outlet for repressed depression and anger created a ticking time bomb within Hansen.

Hansen showed several mental illnesses early on in his criminal career. In a trial transcript from one of his early arrests, his mental state is discussed as an issue with his release and further need for evaluation and treatment:

Although the current offense is Hansen's first for theft, he informed the examining psychiatrists that he had an episodic stealing problem. In 1976, Dr. Parker wrote a second evaluation letter in which he characterizes Hansen's stealing as "probably obsessive" because Hansen "has an inability to resist it and a feeling of being forced." Hansen began therapy with Dr. Robert McManmon who diagnosed Hansen's illness as a bipolar affective disorder which is a variant of a manic-depressive disorder. Dr. McManmon, testifying at Hansen's sentencing hearing, distinguished Hansen's disorder from the classic manic-depressive pattern by the absence of any serious depressive episodes. Hansen's impulses were poorly controlled during the mood and energy upswings of this disorder. During manic episodes sufferers of this disease tend to develop an abnormal preoccupation (mania) toward some activity. Kleptomania, the impulse to steal without economic need, is a manifestation of this illness. Dr. McManmon further testified that Hansen's prior offenses were also likely manifestations of his disorder. The type of behavior indicated by those convictions is "known to occur in this disorder as one of the expressions of the poorly controlled behavior."

Although in 1971 Dr. Parker wrote that it would be difficult to treat Hansen's disorder, the drug lithium has since become acceptable treatment for controlling manic episodes. Lithium checks a patient's manic behavior until he can learn to control himself. Since lithium controls rather than cures, Dr. McManmon stated that complete assurances for Hansen's future behavior were impossible. However, he noted that Hansen had stabilized on lithium, had developed a good rapport with Dr. McManmon, and meaningful therapy had begun so that he "wouldn't anticipate any problems with [Hansen] continuing treatment now." Dr. McManmon believed that the best safeguard against further expression of the illness was continued treatment and it was preferable to have Hansen remain an active member of society. The prognosis was favorable.

The judge himself pointed out Hansen's inability to function in society:

The court, remarking upon the difficulty of the case, described and applied the State v. Chaney, 477 P.2d 441 (Alaska 1970), sentencing criteria. As to rehabilitation potential, Hansen had no

31

trade or educational deficiencies to remedy. His problem was psychiatric. Were rehabilitation the only consideration, the judge stated that he would have granted probation with strict conditions regarding therapy and lithium treatment. Nevertheless, he feared that Hansen was dangerous during manic episodes, and thought that he should be isolated from society. Furthermore, the court believed that the goal of deterrence would only be achieved by a term of incarceration in order to provide Hansen with an "incentive to cooperate" and in recognition of the fact that this offense was Hansen's third felony conviction.

And yet, despite these factors, Hansen not only went back into society unhindered, he quickly stopped taking lithium and receiving treatment for his mental health.

Hansen was diagnosed with an antisocial personality disorder referred to as bipolar disorder. According to the website Psychology Today,

Antisocial personality disorder is characterized by a pattern of disregard for and violation of the rights of others. The diagnosis of antisocial personality disorder is not given to individuals under the age of 18 but is given only if there is a history of some symptoms of conduct disorder before age 15.

The symptoms of antisocial personality disorder can vary in severity. The more egregious, harmful, or dangerous behavior patterns are referred to as sociopathic or psychopathic. There has been much debate as to the distinction between these descriptions. Sociopathy is chiefly characterized as something severely wrong with one's conscience; psychopathy is characterized as a complete lack of conscience regarding others. Some professionals describe people with this constellation of symptoms as "stone cold" to the rights of others. Complications of this disorder include imprisonment, drug abuse, and alcoholism.

People with this illness may seem charming on the surface, but they are likely to be irritable and aggressive as well as irresponsible. They may have numerous somatic complaints and perhaps attempt suicide. Due to their manipulative tendencies, it is difficult to tell whether they are lying or telling the truth.

This term is used as a blanket term for people who suffer from sudden personality splits and changes, impulse control issues, and the inability to feel societally appropriate emotions. Numerous witnesses described Hansen's sudden emotional changes. Cindy Paulson spoke of how he went from a shy and polite man to suddenly turning red, becoming angry, and seeming to almost become someone else. Officers present when the information confirming Hansen's involvement in the murders came in said he seemed to transform. His face turned red, his lips screwed into an angry snarl, and his eyes blazed.

The *Alaska Dispatch* had an article regarding this change:

Rothschild recounted watching Hansen transform into "the monster he was" the day prosecutors sat down with Hansen and laid out the evidence against him. They told Hansen they had seized his map marked with 17 locations, spots that they believed indicated the locations of bodies.

"He was mild-mannered Bob the Baker, and as I'm looking at him, all of sudden he transformed. The hair on the back of his neck stood up and his neck got red, and he was pissed," Rothschild said in a phone interview Thursday.

"I can still see him when he got livid like that," he said.

Hansen asked to speak with his attorneys and went out into another room. "You could hear him screaming at his lawyers," Rothschild said.

Hansen didn't see his victims as human, the attorney said. "In his mind there were good girls and bad girls."

How Hansen saw himself and his victims was one of the more chilling aspects of his confession. In the excerpt below (part of a marathon 12-hour interview), he responds to questions from District Attorney Krumm and Detective Flothe.

KRUMM: Why did you drive out to the road, instead of just going to a hotel or motel in town?

HANSEN: You know if you go to a motel or something with it, it's more or less like a prostitution deal. I'm going and, or I'd—I guess I'm trying to even convince myself maybe I wasn't really buying sex, it was being given to me, in the aspect that I was good enough that it was being given to me. Uh, if I can explain that a little bit better gentlemen. Going back in my life, way back to my high school days and so forth, I was, I guess what you might call very frustrated, upset all the time. I would see my friends and so forth going out on dates and so forth and had a tremendous desire to do the same thing. From the scars and so forth on my face you can probably see, I could see why girls wouldn't want to get close to me and when I'm nervous and upset like this here; if I, I'll try to demonstrate if I can think about exactly what I'm going to say and if I talk slow I can keep myself from stuttering. But at the time during my junior high or high school days I could not control my speech at all. I was always so embarrassed and upset with it from people making fun of me that I hated the word school, I guess this is why I burned down the bus way back in Iowa ... I can remember going up and talking to someone, man or woman, classmate or whatever and start to say something and start to stutter so badly that especially in the younger years I would run away crying, run off someplace and hide for a day or so. The worst there was that I was the rebuttal of all the girls around the school and so forth. The jokes. If I could have faced it, I know now if I could have faced it and laughed along with them it would have stopped but I couldn't at the time and it just, it got so it controlled me, I didn't control it. I didn't start to hate all women, as a matter of fact I would venture to say I started to fall in love with every one of them. Every one of them become so precious to me 'cause I wanted their—I wanted their friendship … I wanted them to like me so much. On top of things that have happened, I don't want to, I'm not saying that I hate all women, I don't. Quite to the contrary, if, I guess in my own mind what I'm classifying is a good woman, not a prostitute. I'd do everything in my power, any way, shape or form to do anything for her and to see that no harm ever came to her, but I guess prostitutes are women I'm putting down as lower than myself. I don't know if I'm making sense or not. And you know, when this started to happen I wanted—you know … It happened the first time there, you know, and I went home and I was literally sick to my stomach … Over the years I've gone in many many topless and bottomless bars in town and so forth and never, never touched one of the girls in there in any way, shape, or form until they asked. It's like, it's like it was a game—they had to pitch the ball before I could bat. They had to approach me first saying about I get off at a certain time, we could go out and have a good time, or something like this here. If they don't, we weren't playing the game right. They had to approach me. I've talked to, I suppose I made it a point to try to talk to, every girl in there. Sometimes if I thought there was a possibility that she didn't say it the first time but she might come back and say it again, now I've invited two or three table dances with her and comment to her how nice she looked and everything else and I try to keep it in a joking tone, "Gosh you know, you sure would be some thing, you know, for later on," but that's as far as it would go until she, then she had to make, I guess play out my fantasy. She had to come out and say we could do it but it's going to cost you some money. Then she was no longer—I guess what you might call a decent girl. I didn't look down at the girls dancing, what the hell they're just trying to make a buck.

FLOTHE: But when they propositioned you, then it made things different?

HANSEN: Then, yes.

35

Most people immediately wonder if a serial killer is a psychopath or a sociopath. The truth is that they aren't always either one, but if anything, Hansen had sociopathic tendencies. Sociopaths can feel emotion; it is just not always what is considered the appropriate emotion for a situation. Hansen, for example, saw his victims as no more than a means to an end, as things rather than people. This is the aspect of his personality that clearly shows sociopathic tendencies.

Hansen was clinically diagnosed with bipolar affective disorder with periods of psychosis. The National Institute of Mental Health explains bipolar disorder as follows:

Bipolar disorder, also known as manic-depressive illness, is a brain disorder that causes unusual shifts in mood, energy, activity levels, and the ability to carry out day-to-day tasks.

There are four basic types of bipolar disorder; all of them involve clear changes in mood, energy, and activity levels. These moods range from periods of extremely "up," elated, and energized behavior (known as manic episodes) to very sad, "down," or hopeless periods (known as depressive episodes). Less severe manic periods are known as hypomanic episodes.

Bipolar I Disorder—defined by manic episodes that last at least 7 days, or by manic symptoms that are so severe that the person needs immediate hospital care. Usually, depressive episodes occur as well, typically lasting at least 2 weeks. Episodes of depression with mixed features (having depression and manic symptoms at the same time) are also possible.

Bipolar II Disorder—defined by a pattern of depressive episodes and hypomanic episodes, but not the full-blown manic episodes described above.

Cyclothymic Disorder (also called cyclothymia)—defined by numerous periods of hypomanic symptoms as well numerous periods of depressive symptoms lasting for at least 2 years (1 year in children and adolescents). However, the symptoms do not meet the diagnostic requirements for a hypomanic episode and a depressive episode.

Other Specified and Unspecified Bipolar and Related Disorders— defined by bipolar disorder symptoms that do not match the three categories listed above.

People with bipolar disorder experience periods of unusually intense emotion, changes in sleep patterns and activity levels, and unusual behaviors. These distinct periods are called "mood episodes." Mood episodes are drastically different from the moods and behaviors that are typical for the person. Extreme changes in energy, activity, and sleep go along with mood episodes.

Sometimes a mood episode includes symptoms of both manic and depressive symptoms. This is called an episode with mixed features. People experiencing an episode with mixed features may feel very sad, empty, or hopeless, while at the same time feeling extremely energized.

Bipolar disorder can be present even when mood swings are less extreme. For example, some people with bipolar disorder experience hypomania, a less severe form of mania. During a hypomanic episode, an individual may feel very good, be highly productive, and function well. The person may not feel that anything is wrong, but family and friends may recognize the mood swings and/or changes in activity levels as possible bipolar disorder. Without proper treatment, people with hypomania may develop severe mania or depression.

Stories of Hansen's life have focused on the stark difference between the face he presented to the community—that of a quiet family man—and the angry murderer whose face was seen only by his victims. What he was like at home, when not killing or putting on a front for other people, is unknown. It is very possible he had periods of depression. Often those who do find solace in the solitude offered by activities like hunting and fishing. Hansen's insecurity and lack of self-confidence bolster the theory that he suffered from depression. He often sent his family away on trips and vacations. One reason for this was that it left him free to hunt and prey on women, but it may also have further enabled his withdrawn personality.

Bipolar disorder is genetic and is a physiologically determinable feature. A chemical imbalance and possible changes to certain aspects of the brain enhance the issues and behavior-causing parts of the human psyche. Although Hansen apparently had no severe trauma in his childhood, he did lack positive reinforcement and love. There was a heavy focus on discipline and physical labor, compounded by his inability to fit in with children his age. His stability declined further in his teen years as his pastime of killing animals and setting fires compensated for the cruel and/or dismissive way his classmates treated him. A study published in the *British Journal of Psychiatry* discusses how such traumas force a negative progression in bipolar-prone children:

Within affective disorder, the relationship between childhood events and psychosis appears to be relatively symptom-specific. It is possible that the pathways leading to psychotic symptoms differ, with delusions and non-hallucinatory symptoms being influenced less by childhood or early environmental experience.

In recent years a number of studies have investigated an association between the presence of psychotic symptoms and a history of childhood trauma. A recent meta-analysis of 36 studies concluded childhood adversity increases the risk of psychosis nearly three-fold. Some authors now propose a causal relationship between these early childhood events and the subsequent development of schizophrenia and this association has influenced key cognitive models of psychosis. One example is the proposal that adverse experiences in childhood will lead to the development of negative schemas of the self and the world (the self as vulnerable and others as dangerous) that facilitate the development of paranoid delusions. Furthermore, Birchwood et al suggest that childhood experience of social adversity leads to the development of negative schemas involving social humiliation and subordination, which in turn may fuel paranoia. Alternatively, it is proposed within biological models of schizophrenia that the experience of abuse creates vulnerability to psychosis through heightened stress reactivity and cortisol dysfunction. In addition, affective dysfunction following childhood trauma is increasingly highlighted as a mechanism through which psychosis develops.

However, this analysis, and much of the literature to date, focuses on non-affective psychosis or data from population-based studies with subclinical psychotic-like experiences. We know that childhood trauma is also associated with a wide number of adverse outcomes, for example depression, suicidal behavior, personality disorder and bipolar disorder. Affective dysfunction is also proposed as a mechanism to explain these associations. For example, Etain et al suggest that a dual role of genetic and environmental influences of socially and morally inappropriate rewards and parental attitudes during childhood induces affective dysregulation in the developing child that precedes the development of bipolar disorder. Thus, given that childhood trauma is proposed as a risk factor for psychosis and affective dysfunction, it is surprising that few studies have investigated the role of childhood trauma in psychotic symptoms as part of an affective disorder to date. In addition, childhood trauma itself encompasses many experiences, but few studies have investigated specific life events in detail. Bentall et al looked at this issue in a large population-based sample and found that sexual abuse was associated only with hallucinations, whereas being brought up in institutional care was associated with 'paranoia'. They proposed the specific associations observed were consistent with current psychological theories about the origins of hallucinations and paranoia. Our study sought to build and expand the current evidence base by exploring the association between a range of adverse childhood events and the presence of psychotic symptoms in a very large, well-characterized sample of patients with bipolar disorder. We hypothesized that for individuals with affective disorder, childhood trauma would show a significant association with psychosis, and in particular with psychotic symptoms coupled with dysregulation of mood (i.e. mood congruent delusions and hallucinations) and with persecutory or abusive content.

Their results focused on the heightened possibility of psychotic episodes, often displayed inwardly as self-harm and suicide or outwardly as violent tendencies. Hansen's psychosis was the latter, an outward expression of primal violence and destruction of the women he hunted and harmed.

At his arson trial, Hansen was initially determined to have psychosis as a byproduct of bipolar disorder and antisocial behavior. The treatment was lithium, a common medication used to help stabilize the chemical balance and therefore the mood of those with bipolar disorder and manic episodes. According to the website of the Virtual Medical Centre,

Lithium has for a long time been the gold standard for mood stabilization. It is effective in both manic and depressive episodes and for long term maintenance therapy. The most common side effects include slight shaking of the hands, thirst, queasiness (usually goes away after some time), headache, tiredness, irregular pulse, loss of appetite, weight gain, bloating and muscle weakness. When a patient is placed on lithium treatment their doctor will do routine blood tests.

Hansen, however, was not monitored after his release and quickly stopped taking his medication. Every time he committed a crime and was caught, the psychological evaluations came to the same conclusion: antisocial personality disorder consisting of bipolar affective disorder with psychosis and manic episodes of violence.

He was considered a danger to society, and yet somehow he was always released.

It's hard to say whether Hansen would have followed the criminal path he did if he had been properly treated or even institutionalized. The problem with evaluating some psychiatric disorders is that the person learns how to put on a mask, how to function in society without drawing attention to their darker side. For Hansen, this wasn't entirely the case. He had a multitude of rape victims trying to report him, and he had a criminal past. Instead, there were two other factors that allowed him to continue on for so long. First were the failings of a system that determined him to be a threat and yet refused to incarcerate or institutionalize him. Second was his decision to hunt and prey upon societal outcasts—prostitutes and strippers, women who were down on their luck, living a high-risk lifestyle. Some had a history of drug abuse, many had no family or friends in Anchorage, and most who survived knew that police wouldn't take them seriously or feared that Hansen would come after them if he were arrested.

Hansen was not the stereotypically suave, intelligent, and emotionless serial killer of Hollywood lore. He had a temper, was emotionally unstable, and was even rather sloppy in his work. And yet he was able to murder at least 17 women and rape several dozen more. Regardless of his psychological difficulties, he was well aware that what he was doing was wrong, and yet he persisted. He denied his activities and covered them up. He was clinically sane, but very disturbed.

Those Who Fell Prey

Although Robert Hansen is known for raping and killing prostitutes, some of his victims were ordinary women who simply found themselves outside in one of the "stalking grounds" where he would drive in circles looking for a target. The FBI lists Hansen as having killed 17 women and raped 30. The information is far from certain, though. The red X's that Hansen marked on his aviation map corresponded to the locations of his victims' bodies. A majority of the X's checked out, confirming that Hansen had indeed committed some of the murders in which he was denying guilt. Because most of the locations were in wilderness areas such as parks and forests, however, it would have been easy for wild animals and the elements to remove most, if not all, traces of the victims who weren't found. This, then, is the list of the 17 deceased and 1 escaped victims of Hansen that the FBI has evidence, circumstantial or physical, to confirm. Hansen's modus operandi was very consistent in all cases where the victims were identified, and thus the circumstantial evidence of him hunting in the areas where bodies were not recovered was often convincing enough to the authorities.

Celia "Beth" Van Zanten (17 or 18 years old)
Missing: December 23, 1971
Discovered: December 25, 1971
Location Found: McHugh Creek State Park

Celia Van Zanten, known as Beth, had a difficult home life. She had two brothers and a "foster cousin" by the name of Greg. Her brothers spent most of their time lying around the house, usually high, and her "cousin" liked to frequent bars and clubs and was usually intoxicated. On December 23, 1971, Beth walked to a convenience store and never returned.

On December 25, 1971, Christmas Day, two brothers, Gary and Dennis Lawler, were making a road trip to photograph the winter scenes of Alaska when they stopped at McHugh Creek State Park. The park was a section of wilderness where two ridges intersected with McHugh Creek. Near one of the picnic areas was a waterfall that Dennis wanted to get a bigger angle on for a photograph. In order to capture the scene, he had to climb down a ledge that overlooked the bank of the river. As he prepared to take the perfect shot, his eyes glanced over what looked like a mannequin behind a bush. She was naked from the waist down, lying in the snow at an awkward angle. Dennis returned to his brother Gary and told him what he had seen, and they left to find a phone and call police.

Sergeant Walter Gilmour, an Alaska state trooper, ended up taking the call. At the scene, investigators noted that the woman was young with pale skin and long, light blonde hair. She matched the description of the missing teenager Celia "Beth" Van Zanten. Her body showed signs of sexual molestation, and her chest and torso had been cut up with a knife. Wire had been used to bind her wrists behind her. Taking into consideration the distance from the ledge behind her, the position of her body, and the prevailing temperatures, authorities theorized that she had been running from the parking lot above when she fell off the ledge and proceeded to crawl away. She had eventually frozen to death in the single-digit temperatures. Investigators did find tire marks in the parking lot that suggested someone had circled around several times, but as they searched the scene, it began raining, quickly destroying any usable prints. They did find a silver belt buckle, a black belt, and yellow tissue paper nearby, but nothing else.

Beth's relatives were inebriated when police interviewed them, making their testimony both contradictory and unreliable. Greg had the most suspicious story; he claimed that he had come by before Beth went missing, but her brothers didn't remember seeing him. However, multiple sightings of Greg extremely intoxicated in public (which had resulted in police involvement) during the relevant time period gave him an alibi. Neighborhood witnesses did recall seeing Beth hitchhiking at around 11 PM the night she went missing. No one had seen who picked her up, though, or had any more information.

Then Sergeant Gilmour received information from an informant who had an idea as to what had occurred the night Beth disappeared. Sandra Patterson was an 18-year-old heroin addicted prostitute who also happened to be the daughter of a state trooper. While she was in the Nevada Club parking lot on December 18, a man came up to her with a gun and demanded that she go with him. She told Sergeant Gilmour that he had tied her hands with leather shoelaces and forced her to strip as he drove. He pulled over and attempted to have sex with her on multiple occasions, but she persuaded him not to do so in the car. He eventually took her to a motel out on the Kenai Peninsula. He raped her, but was unable to satisfy himself. Sandra told Sergeant Gilmour that she tried to be as passive as possible. He had hit her once in anger, and she was afraid of what he was going to do to her. Before releasing her, he drove into the woods and warned her that if she told anyone he would kill her.

The culprit was described as mid to late 20s, a bit taller than five and a half feet, skinny, awkward, with dark hair and glasses. In the 70s, criminal records had not generally been computerized; instead, police had what was often referred to as an "asshole book" consisting of mug shots and photographs of known sexual deviants. It included predators, assault suspects, and rape suspects both convicted and not. Sandra Patterson thumbed through the pages and stopped on a photograph of Hansen, absolutely certain that he was the man who had kidnapped her. The incident had occurred while Hansen was awaiting trial for pulling a gun on a woman in traffic. However, Sandra had dropped the charges when she became scared that he wouldn't be convicted and would kill her.

Although Hansen denied involvement in Celia Van Zanten's murder when he was arrested, he did slip up when talking with investigators later. When they mentioned the location where her body had been found, he immediately recalled who it was—but then backtracked, saying that he remembered them trying to pin it on him when he was in trouble for Sandra Patterson's rape. Due to the nature of the crime, the slashed bra strap, the bindings, the partially undressed state, the wilderness location, and the fact that Celia's home was in one of Hansen's stalking areas, authorities were confident that he was responsible for her death. But he was never charged for any crime against Celia Van Zanten.

Megan Emerick (17 years old)
Missing: July 7, 1973
Discovered: Still Missing
Location: Last seen in Seward, Alaska

Megan Emerick was a native of Delta Junction, Alaska. She was an outdoors enthusiast and a student at the Seward Skill Center, later renamed the Alaska Vocational Technical Center. She had no known connection to sex work and simply seems to have been in the wrong place at the wrong time—in her case, leaving a laundromat at her dormitory on July 7, 1973. She had brown hair and hazel eyes and was last seen wearing a long-sleeved shirt with a white checkered pattern under a brown short-sleeve sweater, jeans, and ski boots.

Hansen denied involvement in Megan Emerick's disappearance, claiming that he didn't pick up women in Seward:

Anchorage DA Vic Krumm: "Way back in the early '70s, there were a number of young women from Seward..."

Hansen: "Ah... out of Seward gentlemen, I never had anything... anything to do with any girls out of Seward."

This was later contradicted when he admitted to the kidnapping and murder of Joanne Messina. Megan lived less than 11 minutes from where Joanne Messina was picked up, near a dock where Hansen kept a boat and often visited other fishermen. In September of 2008, two former cellmates of Hansen came forward claiming to have information about some of the women Hansen denied kidnapping and murdering. They said that they had a map with the grave locations of some of the women, and that Megan was one of them, but they refused to hand it over unless unrelated charges against them were dropped. Due to the nature of their crimes and the fact that Hansen had already been jailed for life, authorities declined the deal.

Mary K. Thill (23 years old)
Missing: July 5, 1975
Discovered: Still Missing
Location: Believed to be near Resurrection Bay

Mary Thill was a married woman who asked some friends to give her a ride into town on July 5, 1975. She was last seen at a waterfall near Lowell Point Road between 1:30 and 2:00 PM. Her husband, a worker at Alaska's North Slope, reported her missing when she never came back home. When questioned about her disappearance after his arrest, Hansen told authorities that although he had been in the area at the time she went missing, he was not involved. Mary had light skin, red hair, blue eyes, and wore pink glasses. Her friends said that when they last saw her she was wearing jeans and hiking boots with a gray sweater and an army jacket and carrying a black backpack.

Roxanne Easland (24 years old)
Missing: June 28, 1980
Discovered: Still Missing
Location: 4th Avenue, Anchorage
Also Known As: Roxanne Eastland/Eastlund, Karen Lee Baunsgard, Robin Lee Easland

Roxanne Easland was a well-known prostitute in Anchorage. For two weeks prior to her disappearance, Roxanne had been living with her boyfriend in the Budget Motel on Spenard Road. On June 28, 1980, Roxanne was using the name Karen Lee Baunsgard when she left to meet a client. The meeting was to be in a downtown hotel on 4th Avenue. She was never seen again.

Hansen did admit to kidnapping and murdering Roxanne Easland. Her body, though, was not recovered, even with the use of Hansen's marked aviation map. Her remains may have been disturbed or carried away by wild animals.

"Eklutna Annie" (16 to 25 years old)
Missing: Unknown—possibly Hansen's first murder victim
Discovered: July 21, 1980
Location: Eklutna Road

One of Hansen's unidentified victims, whom he admitted to murdering, was dubbed "Eklutna Annie." Her remains were found by county workers in a shallow grave in a heavily wooded area on Eklutna Lake Road. Her body was badly decomposed and had been severely damaged by wild animals. The evidence at the scene suggested she had been wearing red knee-high high-heeled boots, jeans, a leather jacket and a sleeveless knit top. Gold twisted loop earrings, a copper bangle with turquoise stones, a turquoise-and-shell necklace with a heart pendant, a white-and-brown shell ring, a gold Timex ladies' wristwatch, and a pack of Salem brand matches were also found on her body.

Hansen told police she was a prostitute or topless dancer. He described all his victims this way, but Eklutna Annie's clothing suggests that it was probably true in this case. He also told them he believed she was from a village called Kodiak, but that has not been confirmed, although she was a mixed-race Native American.

Hansen told police he had picked her up and taken her out into the woods in his truck. When she got away from him and ran, he chased her down. Eventually he was able to grab a hold of her hair and pull her back, at which point she pulled a knife from her purse and attempted to defend herself. Hansen said he got the knife away from her, stabbed her in the back and then left her there.

Her remains are currently in the Anchorage Memorial Park under a bronze plaque engraved with "Jane Doe, Died 1980." Authorities believe that she was Hansen's first murder victim.

Joanne (Joanna) Messina (24 years old)
Missing: July 1980
Discovered: July 1980
Location: Near Eklutna Road

As well as an accomplished hunter, Hansen was an avid fisherman. In the 1970s he had a large boat that he kept moored in Seward. He would travel there with his camper and go on fishing trips. "In the spring I would take my boat and pickup and camper and drive to Seward and leave it, then just drive a car back and forth [from Anchorage]," Hansen said in his confession. After his arrest, he told authorities that he had often trolled for victims while walking along the Seward shorefront (although he later denied killing some of the victims he allegedly picked up from the area).

One of the women he noticed was Joanne Messina, who worked at a cannery and as a topless dancer. Some sources say she had previously been a nurse. In July of 1980, Joanne was walking to work at the cannery when Hansen approached her. He tried to get her to go back to his camper, but she refused, not wanting to be late to her job. Hansen said, "I met her and I talked to her and... I had my boat down there and was talking [to] her that I was going to go out, out the next day fishing and so forth, would she like to go along, you know." When she politely declined, Hansen pulled out a gun and forced her to go with him. She was raped and killed out near Eklutna Road. Hansen then left her body in a gravel pit not far from where Eklutna Annie was found.

When Joanne's body was found and the state troopers were called in, they were warned that a large bear had been seen in the area. Arriving on the scene, officers confirmed that the body showed signs of having been gnawed on by a large animal. While they were examining it, the bear returned. They tried to shoo it away so they could recover the evidence, but the bear refused to back down. Since it was a protected species, they couldn't shoot it, even as it began to get hostile. Fortunately, the bear calmed down and left after a while, and the troopers were able to collect the body and what was left of the evidence.

Police initially focused on a different suspect in the murder of Joanne Messina. The man was apprehended and brought in for questioning. He denied murdering Joanne, but he failed the polygraph. Detective Chuck Miller, who was leading the investigation, believed this man was the killer. He was therefore a bit annoyed when Detective Flothe put Joanne Messina on his list of victims of the Alaskan serial killer. Flothe's reasoning was that she was a part-time sex worker, was left near where another victim had been left, was killed in the same manner as other victims, and overall met the MO for his killer. Later, when Hansen was arrested, Joanne Messina was one of the four women he admitted to murdering, and he knew enough about the crime scene and evidence to substantiate this admission.

Lisa Futrell (41 years old)
Missing: September 6, 1980
Discovered: May 9, 1984
Location: South of Old Knik Bridge

There isn't much information on Lisa Futrell, but it is known that she was either a prostitute or a topless dancer. Her body was found south of the Old Knik Bridge and was confirmed as one of Hansen's victims; she was one of the marks on his map.

Sherry Morrow (23 years old)
Missing: November 17, 1981
Discovered: September 12, 1982
Location: Banks of the Knik River

An exotic dancer at the Wild Cherry Bar, Sherry Morrow did what she needed to make money. Unfortunately, that often involved using her body. She had a penchant for fast cash, and that weakness put her directly into harm's way. According to the Wild Cherry's manager, "She was really gullible. She could be talked into anything. When I heard [she'd been killed] I thought, gosh, it was almost inevitable."

On November 17, 1981, Sherry was at a friend's house when she said she was leaving to meet a client at Alice's 210 Cafe. The client, a photographer, had promised her $300 to pose nude for a series of photographs. Her client turned out to be Hansen, who later admitted to kidnapping, raping, and killing Sherry Morrow and explained in detail what he did to her.

When Sherry got into Hansen's car, he immediately handcuffed her and used an Ace bandage to blindfold her. He then forced her into the back seat and made her kneel on the floorboard. Hansen drove out to the Knik River. When he tried to remove her handcuffs, Sherry began to fight back. She kicked and screamed, trying to attack Hansen and get away. Hansen retrieved his semi-automatic rifle from the trunk, then sat down and waited, hoping she would calm down. Sherry charged at Hansen, still screaming and trying to attack him. He told police, "I just pointed the Mini-14 up toward her and pulled the trigger."

Hansen took Sherry's arrowhead necklace before digging a shallow grave. He put both Sherry Morrow and the .223 shell casings into the grave. Hunters found the body almost a year later. She had three gunshot wounds in her back from a .223 rifle. Although she was fully dressed, there were no bullet holes in her clothing. Investigators believed that she had been raped and was still naked when she was shot, but was then redressed afterward, before she was buried.

"Perhaps it was both naïveté and greed that doomed Sherry Morrow when she left with Hansen in November 1981."— *Anchorage Daily News*

Andrea Altiery (24 years old)
Missing: December 2, 1981
Discovered: Still Missing
Location: Knik River

Andrea Altiery was last seen by her roommate in their apartment. The exotic dancer was leaving to meet a client for either a photography session or a shopping spree at the Boniface Mall (there are two different accounts as to why she was meeting Hansen). Hansen told police what happened after she was in his car.

As with previous victims, Hansen handcuffed her and blindfolded her before driving to a secluded location next to the Knik River railroad bridge. Trying to keep Andrea under control, Hansen told her that he habitually kidnapped and raped women. He said that he'd last done so a week before, in that very spot, and had let her go because she had cooperated. Andrea accordingly did as he

52

asked. He held a gun to her head and forced her to perform oral sex on him while he fondled her.

Eventually, Andrea told Hansen she needed to use the bathroom. Hansen let her get out of the car. He put the pistol on the hood and turned away to urinate. A noise behind him caused him to turn around as Andrea reached for his pistol. He grabbed it before she could and she attacked him, clawing at his face and eyes. Hansen shot her dead. Andrea was wearing a necklace with a fish charm, and Hansen took it, as well as a pearl ring she had. Then he grabbed a bag from his car and filled it with rocks and gravel. He tied the bag around Andrea's neck and pushed both her and the bag into the river. Her body was never found.

Sue Luna (23 years old)
Missing: May 26, 1982
Discovered: April 24, 1984
Location: Knik River

Sue Luna had a rough life before she moved to Alaska. Her husband was abusive and spent many years in prison for murder. Like many at the time, she hoped that she could make some money off of the influx of people moving to Alaska during the oil boom. Working as a topless dancer at the Good Times Bar, and occasionally as a prostitute, Sue didn't realize she had jumped out of the frying pan and into the fire.

Like several other victims, Sue Luna had been promised $300 to do something for a man she was to meet at Alice's 210 Cafe. On May 26, 1982, Sue told her roommate that she was leaving for that appointment. She didn't return, and the roommate and Sue's sister reported her missing four days later.

According to police, Sue Luna was stripped, blindfolded and sent running through the woods near the Knik River. She was shot multiple times in the back before being buried next to a parking lot by the Knik River Bridge, where she was found two years later.

On a website for the friends and families of murder victims, a friend of Sue's left this message:

Sue was a beautiful person, a loving friend with a heart of gold. Her smile could light up a room. Sue could turn your very worst day, into your best, just by being there and talking things out. She had a zest for life, and a deep love for people.

We do not know the exact date of Sue's death. Robert Hansen, Alaska's Serial Killer, took Sue out to the Knik River in Alaska, stripped her, and made her run like an animal while he hunted her down, and eventually killing her. He shot her to death. He did the same to 16 other women. Her death was in 1983. I've never gotten over it, and I never will.

Once in a lifetime, a true friend comes along, that makes your day brighter, and your life better. Sue loved to laugh. She was a clown, always making faces, or imitating Mick Jagger of the Rolling Stones. She would poke her lips out and pretend to be singing "Satisfaction." She would do this until I was literally doubled over with laughter.

I miss her so much, I miss her friendship and love. It has been 17 years since Sue died, and it feels like yesterday in my heart. I have wonderful memories of my friend who made my life so much better, and I will keep them always. I know Sue is in Heaven, looking down on the people she loved and cared for. She will always be remembered.

He killed my friend, but he could never kill my memories of Sue Luna.
Love and miss you Sue
Reva H.

Paula Goulding (31 years old—possibly 21 according to some records)
Missing: April 24, 1983
Discovered: September 2, 1983
Location: Bank of the Knik River

Paula Goulding was a stripper at the Great Alaska Bush Company in Anchorage. The 31-year-old from Kona, Hawaii, had originally moved to Fairbanks and worked as a secretary before relocating to Anchorage to take up dancing. She was rather new to the club scene and had only just transitioned from dancing topless to dancing nude in order to make more money. She met Hansen on her first night of dancing completely nude. He offered her $200 to meet him for a lunch date, telling her to arrive in a cab. On April 24, 1983, Paula's roommate saw her leave their apartment. When she wasn't back after four days, she called and reported her missing.

On September 2 or 3, 1983, Paula Goulding's body was found in a shallow grave near the Knik River, not far from where another body had been found the previous month. Examining the body, investigators came to the conclusion that she had been bound and blindfolded, raped, and had been running for some time before being shot several times in the back with a .223 caliber rifle. She had then been redressed and buried; the shell casings were thrown in with the body. At first investigators did not think that Paula and Sherry Morrow had been murdered by the same person, but the shell casings found with their bodies were later matched.

After his arrest, Hansen admitted to killing Paula Goulding and explained what had happened to her. He said he had taken her at gunpoint to his plane and flown her out to a cabin where he tied her up, blindfolded her, raped her, and tortured her for quite some time. He then released her and opened the cabin door, pushing her out so she would take off running. He grabbed his rifle and went after her, hunting her down and eventually killing her. He then redressed the body and buried it before going back home.

Paula is buried in the Anchorage Memorial Park Cemetery.

Cindy Paulson (17 years old)
Missing: June 13, 1983
Discovered: Escaped
Location: Merrill Field

Cindy Paulson is not Hansen's only surviving rape victim, but she is the only one known to have escaped after he decided to kill her rather than being released. Hansen picked her up on June 13, 1983, then handcuffed her and took her to his home, where he raped and tortured her for hours before chaining her neck to a post in the basement and taking a nap. When he woke, he took Cindy to Merrill Field, where he had his plane. Cindy escaped while he was busy loading supplies into the aircraft.

She was able to flag down a trucker who took her to a nearby motel. Cindy called her boyfriend and went to the motel where he was staying; the trucker called the police. At first, they weren't certain if Cindy was telling the truth. Hansen was questioned and, although her descriptions of his vehicle, home, and plane were spot-on, he was let go when two of his neighbors supplied an alibi. They later recanted when authorities got additional evidence suggesting that Hansen was their killer.

The movie *The Frozen Ground* is based on Cindy Paulson and Detective Glenn Flothe's parts in the investigation into Hansen's crimes. Cindy's report was the reason Detective Flothe became so invested in the case. His dogged response to the attack revealed incidents and police reports from Hansen's past and caused his alibi to be re-evaluated. Unfortunately, as hard as he tried, there were still more deaths before Hansen was finally apprehended and put behind bars.

Malai Larsen (28 years old)
Missing: Unknown
Discovered: April 24, 1984
Location: Near parking lot by the Old Knik Bridge

Not much is known about Malai Larsen other than that her body was found after Hansen admitted to her murder and led authorities to the site.

DeLynn "Sugar" Frey (20 years old)
Missing: April 1983
Discovered: August 25, 1985
Location: Horseshoe Lake or Knik River

DeLynn Frey was a young, blonde prostitute who Hansen flew out to the wilderness in 1983. A native of New Mexico and the mother of a young daughter, she had issues with heroin addiction and ended up taking to the streets in Anchorage, Alaska. Hansen released her nude and blindfolded before shooting her down. He buried her in a shallow grave on a gravel bar either in Horseshoe Lake or the Knik River (sources are unclear). DeLynn was found by a pilot who was out practicing landings on the bar. Even though she was buried with rings her mother recognized, her identity wasn't confirmed until 1990.

Teresa Watson (unknown)
Missing: March 25, 1983
Discovered: April 26, 1984
Location: Scenic Lake on the Kenai Peninsula

Teresa Watson is another victim of whom little is known. However, Hansen admitted to killing her and revealed the location of her body. Teresa was a prostitute who was last seen on March 25, 1983, when she was leaving to meet a client. Hansen said he flew her out to Scenic Lake. After raping and killing her, he tried to bury her, but the ground was still frozen, so he threw her body out of his plane onto the lakeshore. It was discovered a year later, badly damaged by the local wildlife.

Angela Feddern (24 years old)
Missing: February 1983
Discovered: April 26, 1984
Location: Figure Eight Lake in the Susitna Basin

In Fairbanks, Angela Feddern was the mother of a 5-year-old girl; in Anchorage she was a prostitute. Although she was last seen in February of 1983, she wasn't reported missing until May. Her family knew of her shady lifestyle and was used to her disappearing for periods of time. Angela's mother had always feared that her lifestyle would be the end of her; she even told a journalist, "That was the life she chose. Angie just couldn't find it in herself to go out and get a thinking job."

A year after she went missing, Angela's remains were found on the banks of Figure Eight Lake in the Susitna Basin, across from Cook Inlet near Anchorage.

Tamara "Tami" Pederson (20 years old)
Missing: August 1982
Discovered: April 29, 1984
Location: On the banks of the Knik River near Sherry Morrow's body

Tamara Pederson, "Tami," was a stripper at a club in Anchorage. She also worked as a prostitute. In August of 1982, Tami was told she would be paid $200 to model in costumes and naked for a client. She left and was never seen again. Robert Hansen admitted to her murder and helped authorities find her body, which was buried in a shallow grave on the Knik River not far from Sherry Morrow's.

"Horseshoe Harriet" (19-20 years old)
Missing: Unknown
Discovered: April 25, 1984
Location: Horseshoe Lake

Officially labeled as Jane Doe #3 but known to the press as Horseshoe Harriet, this young woman was discovered in skeletal condition on April 25, 1984, in a shallow grave near Horseshoe Lake. As condoms were found with her remains, it was believed that she was a prostitute; however, she didn't match any known missing persons. Damage to her skeleton indicated that she had been stabbed and shot in the back four times each. Investigators concluded that she was another of Hansen's victims who had been running naked through the woods when he hunted her down and killed her.

These are all of Hansen's known and confirmed victims. However, the red X's on his aviation map far outnumbered the murders to which he admitted and the bodies that authorities found. Hansen may have had a cabin somewhere in the Alaskan wilderness, but this has not been confirmed. He did tell investigators that he had a cabin, but recanted later on. No cabin was registered in Hansen's name or linked to him during the investigation. However, one structure has become known as the "Butcher Baker Cabin" and has suffered years of vandalism and stigma despite the lack of a confirmed connection to Hansen. The area around this cabin has been dug up multiple times by people trying to find the remains of more victims.

Many of Hansen's victims were prostitutes and/or strippers, and he referred to all of them as such, but it must be noted that this was not true of all of them. At least two just happened to be walking in the wrong place at the wrong time.

The Trial

Upon his initial arrest, Robert Christian Hansen was charged with insurance fraud and theft, assault, several weapons offenses, and kidnapping. Hansen refused to answer questions and requested an attorney. An Anchorage grand jury indicted Hansen for four cases of first degree assault and kidnapping, five counts of misconduct while using a firearm, second degree theft, and theft by insurance fraud. Murder charges were delayed until the ballistics information on Hansen's guns was returned. Hansen was taken to jail with a bail of over half a million dollars.

As Hansen continued to deny any involvement in the murders—as well as any guilt in the other charges—forensics technicians were working on matching the evidence to Hansen. Ballistics is a form of forensic science that utilizes tiny details in bullets and expended cartridges to find a match with the suspect's weapon. In this case, the comparison was between the .223 cases recovered near the victims and Hansen's .223 caliber Ruger Mini-14 rifle. There were only four murders that could be tied to the weapon definitively: those of Joanne Messina, Sherry Morrow, Eklutna Annie, and Paula Goulding.

Still, with four ballistic confirmations out of 17 known victims, there was no denying that Hansen was the murderer. On top of the jewelry, aviation map, and Hansen's own history with rape and abduction, the case looked rather solid. An article by Paul Sutherland explained how the police set the stage and quickly acquired the evidence to get Hansen locked up before learning more about his crimes:

At 8am on the 27 October 1983, Hansen was arrested at his bakery and was taken to the Anchorage trooper station. There, Flothe had stage-managed an interview room following pointers from the FBI. Hansen was placed in an interview room that had been carefully set out. There were maps of the Knik River along the walls, pictures of the grave sites, the victims, on the desk. There were files and folders with the names of Hansen's family, friends and acquaintances on them. He was left to sit in here alone for a while, in an attempt to make him stew, and was watched by Flothe through a two-way mirror. Hansen appeared more intrigued than concerned. A few minutes later Flothe and Sergeant Darryl Galyan entered the room, and began an interview with Hansen that was to last 5 hours.

Whilst Hansen was being interviewed, a team of officers was searching his house. Behind wooden paneling in his trophy room police found items of cheap jewelry that was later traced back to the dead girls. Police also found a Ruger Mini-14 hunting rifle hidden under floorboards, which was later matched by ballistics as being the weapon that had killed Sherry Morrow and Paula Goulding. The most telling item found was an aviation map of the Anchorage region, which was dotted with 20 drawn on asterisks. Two of these corresponded with sites where bodies had been found, and a third indicated the spot where the body of Joanne Messina, a 24 year old prostitute, was found in July 1980. Investigators later discovered that she had last been seen with a small, stammering man, with a pockmarked face.

Hansen initially denied any connection with the murders, but when confronted with the wealth of evidence against him, decided to confess. He admitted that the asterisks on the map were grave sites of prostitutes that he had murdered. Hansen claimed that he had not killed every girl he had taken up into the wilderness. He claimed that he only wanted oral sex, and if the girls complied, they were flown home. If they resisted, he would force them to strip at gunpoint, and then make them run. They would usually be given a head start, and then Hansen would stalk them like an animal. Chillingly, he would sometimes allow the victim to think she had escaped, but would then track her down and make her run again. This would continue until the victim was too cold and exhausted to continue running, when the victims would be shot. The redressing, Hansen claimed, was to satisfy his need for control and he likened it to a trophy.

Hansen had his lawyer meet with District Attorney Krumm to make a deal. Hansen agreed to plead guilty to the four murders and tell authorities where the other bodies were if they didn't charge him for the other 13 murders. Knowing that the sentence for four murders would be more than enough to keep Hansen in jail for the rest of his life, the DA agreed.

Hansen ended up showing the police a total of 15 graves from his map. Twelve of these were for murders they had not been aware of, and only 11 contained bodies. There were other markers on his map that they were not able to check for one reason or another, including freezing weather, inaccessible locations, and Hansen's refusal to help.

The search for and retrieval of the bodies of Hansen's victims was an arduous process—at least for the police officers involved. Hansen, however, seemed to enjoy explaining his crimes and what he had done to each victim as they traveled to the sites. He would walk around the crime scenes, almost smiling as he recounted the events.

Although Hansen refused to confirm whether or not he was responsible for many of the disappearances, this is not to say he was uncooperative. He helped detectives uncover where he had buried many of his victims. This was a task Hansen took to with a sickening relish. During a helicopter tour of the gravesites, he would frequently become excited and exhilarated, reliving the murders over and over in his head. Handcuffed, Hansen would plough through chest-high snow drifts and triumphantly point out the grave of one of his victims. Sometimes he would drop to his knees and dig furiously with his bare hands, wild-eyed with a broad grin on his face. By the end of the summer of 1984, 11 bodies had been found, 10 of which were formally identified.

Hansen walked investigators through his "process" as well:

"I pull out the gun—I think the standard speech was, 'Look, you're a professional. You don't get excited, you know there is some risk to what you've been doing. If you do exactly what I tell you, you're not going to get hurt. You're just going to count this off as a bad experience and be a little more careful next time who you are gonna proposition or go out with,' you know. I tried to act as tough as I could, to get them as scared as possible. Give that right away, even before I started talking at all. Reach over, you know, and hold that head back and put a gun in her face and get 'em to feel helpless, scared, right there I'm sure—maybe it's not the same procedure for you—you always try to get control of the situation, so some things don't start going bad, maybe? I've seen some cop shows on TV, I don't know, OK?"

The officers went along with his "show" and gathered as much information as they could. The trial was long, but not as long as it would have been if Hansen had been tried for all 17 murders. When a serial killer is being tried, it's not uncommon for prosecution to be halted before all of the cases have been heard.

One reason is that, after the first few verdicts, the defendant has usually been sentenced to more prison time than he could possibly survive. Further trials would only tie up the courts and cost taxpayers money.

Another reason is the possibility of some or all of the guilty verdicts being overturned. Due to the double jeopardy rule, those cases couldn't be retried; but if prosecutors have kept some murders in reserve, they can file new charges in those to ensure that the killer doesn't escape on a technicality.

The third reason is that a single murder trial can take anywhere from weeks to years, depending on how many loopholes and stays the defense pulls to slow the progress of the case. Multiply that by 17 and the entire process could take a very long time indeed. During this time, the defendant would be held in a less-secure temporary detention facility, increasing escape risk—and he might even die of old age before he ever faced punishment in the penitentiary!

So while Hansen was convicted of just four murders out of the 17 he certainly committed, he was sentenced to 461 years plus life without parole, and prosecutors were more than content with that outcome.

Caging the Hunter

On February 27, 1984, a week after pleading guilty, Robert Hansen went before Superior Court Judge Ralph Moody for sentencing. He had pled to four first-degree murders (Eklutna Annie, Joanna Messina, Paula Goulding, and Sherry Morrow) and unofficially admitted to 13 more. When recounting what he had done, Hansen showed no remorse, fear, sadness, or any emotion other than the odd smile. The judge sentenced him to 461 years plus life without the possibility of parole.

Hansen was first taken to the United States Penitentiary in Lewisburg, Pennsylvania. Part of his agreement was that he be incarcerated in a federal penitentiary rather than a maximum security state prison. Nonetheless, he was moved to the Lemon Creek Correctional Center in Juneau, Alaska, in 1988 and then to the newly-built Spring Creek Correctional Center in Seward, Alaska. He stayed there until he fell ill and was taken to a prison hospital, Alaska Regional Hospital, where he passed away at 1:30 AM on April 21, 2014, at the age of 75.

Several inmates have come forward with information they say Hansen gave them in prison. They claim to know the whereabouts of still-missing victims and about Hansen's involvement in additional murders. However, authorities believe that most of these claims have no basis in fact and are simply attempts to capitalize on the open questions of the Hansen case in exchange for sentence reductions. Furthermore, they have consistently decided not to pursue even potentially valid claims. They have stated that, while they mean no disrespect to the families and victims, they do not see the recovery of bones (if even bones remain by now) as a reason for allowing other criminals to escape their own sentences.

After Hansen's incarceration, the Pope & Young company removed his trophies from their publications. They stated that although his records remained valid, they did not wish to publicize them. Hansen had once stated that hunting the women was like "going after a Dall sheep or a grizzly bear," but this was apparently not an association that Pope & Young wanted to make.

Hansen's wife, Darla, and their two children stayed in Anchorage for a time, but they faced constant scrutiny and harassment. They eventually left Alaska for Arkansas, where they hoped to start life over again in a place where their husband and father was less well known. Darla has only done a handful of interviews.

Alaskan hunters occasionally find bodies in areas that Hansen was known to frequent. These bodies are routinely analyzed to determine if they might belong to one of Hansen's still-missing or unknown victims. There have also been issues with "serial killer tourists" who travel to the scenes where bodies were found. They also dig up areas where bodies were believed to have been dumped but were never discovered. The Big Timber Motel and the privately owned "Butcher Baker Cabin" have suffered from vandals and enthusiasts alike due to Hansen's history.

Several key figures in the investigation had a few choice words, published by the *Alaskan Dispatch*, about the death of Robert Hansen:

"On this day we should only remember his many victims and all of their families and my heart goes out to all of them," wrote Glenn Flothe, retired Alaska State Trooper who was instrumental in Hansen's capture. "As far as Hansen is concerned, this world is better without him," Flothe wrote. "It's a sad day for me, for their families."

"He will not be missed," said Frank Rothschild, the assistant district attorney who tried the case, from Hawaii on Thursday afternoon. "Good riddance to him."

"He's one of those kind of guys that you kind of hope every breath he takes in his life, there's some pain associated with it, because he caused such pain," Rothschild added. "When the Hansen case was over… I was ready," Rothschild said. "It was just so heavy to see what this human being was capable of doing."

Modern Portrayals

Efforts are still being made to identify Horseshoe Harriet and Eklutna Annie. It is also believed that some of Hansen's victims are still unknown. The Alaska State Troopers have information online asking people to help identify the victims and provide any other information regarding the murders and victims of Robert Hansen. Because most of his victims were women down on their luck, drug addicts living on the streets or in rundown apartments and working as prostitutes or strippers, there were often no family members around to claim them. Many of the women were buried in the Anchorage Memorial Cemetery under bronze plaques with their names and dates of birth and death, if known. At the time of Hansen's conviction, one woman held a mass funeral for the victims who had no one come forward to claim them or grieve for them.

There has been a multitude of books, movies, and crime drama episodes based on the Hansen case. The most high profile of them is the movie *The Frozen Ground*, which stars John Cusack as Robert Hansen, Nicholas Cage as Detective Glenn Flothe (renamed Sergeant Jack Holcombe), and Vanessa Hudgens as Cindy Paulson. The movie actually started off as fiction; it was conceived as a more modern twist on the short story "The Most Dangerous Game," the twist being a serial killer who captured people and released them into the wild to hunt them. Then the writer, Scott Walker, learned about Hansen. Here is an excerpt of his interview with Sheila Roberts of Collider:

Scott Walker: I wanted this to be a drama. It has a serial killer in it, which means people call it a serial killer film, but to me it's a drama about this relationship. Why I opened the film the way I did is I wanted the feeling that you are dropped into the middle of this case like it's a bomb going off and then it just ripples. You don't know where the tentacles are going to go and it's going to touch a lot of people and affect them considerably. It's going to wreck lives. I wanted to keep it concise. I didn't want it to be like Zodiac or the stories which have those kinds of [structure]. It could have been thirteen years of titles saying "Six months later and another killing and another body turning up." I just didn't want that. I thought sure, that could tell the story, but that's a documentary as far as I was thinking. I wanted something that was short, intense, and like you were just on the shoulder of these three characters, going into their worlds knowing they're going to collide at some point. It's how and when. That's what you're waiting to find out. It's one of those cases that, to tell it truthfully and honor as many of the facts as I possibly could, Holcombe and Cindy need to meet early on or else there's no story. He doesn't know who the killer is until he meets her. If that happened at the end of Act Two, there are just bodies to be found before then. I wasn't interested in that. There's no relationship going on there. That's just another serial killer film. So, that was the first big decision—that you're going to know very early on who the killer is. And then, it becomes about can he find an overwhelming amount of evidence and how much of it is going to fall away between his fingers in order to get a conviction. And so, that became what the story was about and why I wanted to tell it that way.

Sheila Roberts: How did the finished film compare to what you originally envisioned?

Walker: The script had 275 scenes. I shot 225. That was the reality of when we were two weeks out from starting to shoot. It was like 50 scenes have got to go. And then, I think 30 scenes got cut in the editing to get the time down. The film is about 90 percent of what I envisioned. There are places where it's got more score than I was originally wanting. I always saw it as a drama much more than anything else, and it just has this serial killer element, which means it's getting talked about as a serial killer film. But really, all I mostly was interested in was this relationship. It's a police procedural, but Cindy Paulson is the heart of the film. In the same way as in The Accused, Jody Foster is who the film is about, but some things happen to her, and Kelly McGillis plays what is the backbone of the film. And that's what the police procedural is in this. It's Jack Holcombe's story. He solves the case, but she's the key to it and it's about this relationship between the two of them. I was really pleased that's still in the film, and there are these great moments between the two of them which are based on the reality of when they first met. They didn't go to Skateland [referring to a scene in the film]. They went to Chuck E. Cheese's. She would see moose and bizarre things in the snow.

Roberts: In hindsight, is there anything you wish you had known on the first day of shooting that you discovered later would have been helpful to know?

Walker: I'm sure there is. There are probably hundreds of things I wished I'd known because I knew that on day one. The first shot we did was at 5:00 in the morning, and there was condensed fog and the sun was coming up. It's the shot where John (Cusack) drives down the road. He actually pulls out from behind the school bus, which was intentional imagery of this guy, and pulls into his bakery. I suppose the first learning was that's going to have to be cut because you're never going to be able to have time to use that, and we're just going to have him pulling into the parking lot. All the stuff that I cut out, I don't regret that we went faster to get because I then have the choice. If you don't shoot it, you never have the choice. I was always pushing for more, more, more. We did incredible numbers of set-ups which I didn't realize were incredible until people were saying, "We just did 47 set-ups. That's nuts!" and we were doing that consistently. Literally, every time we did another take, I would remove the cameras and everything because I had to have coverage that I wasn't going to get if I just stayed in the same

73

positions and did takes. That served the film. It was part of the style.

Roberts: What were some of the challenges of writing this and condensing a true story that spans 12 or 13 years into a 2-hour film while also balancing the facts and exploring both sides of the story?

Walker: That is the biggest challenge. The real people were supporting me and helping me with all the information, and I was going after more and more information, and I became overwhelmed with the amount of information that I had. It's the responsibility for whatever ends up in those pages, and if they read it, the worst thing would have been if they go, "This has got nothing to do with what we told you and it's disrespectful." That was the thing, to get the tone right. The only people who I was really concerned about what they thought of the film were the real people. To have feedback from real people that had seen it and they go, "Wow! We're really pleased with the film and think it's terrific. We're really pleased that you were able to stay true to the intent of when we first started talking about what you wanted to do." That's still there. The photos at the end was a big decision.

It was like, "Wow. Is this right or not?" and then going back to the real people and saying, "What do you think because this is about you. I'm just telling your story from another perspective." And then, phoning one of the victim's families and she's saying, "Could you use this photo? That is amazing that my sister will be up there and mentioned because nobody ever mentioned her and she was one of the victims." With stuff like that, you go, "I don't really care what anybody else thinks." I wish I could have tracked down every victim's family but a lot of them didn't use their real names. And a lot of the families don't even know what happened to their daughter. Some of the bodies were never identified so nobody even knows who they are. That's a challenge. But the biggest challenge was how to take 13 years and put it into less than two hours and still have it be true to what happened. You can't tell everything, and you can't have every character, every real person, be in there, because you'd have 30 investigators investigating 30 cases and that would become a mess for an audience to follow.

Walker didn't discuss his decision to rename Detective Glenn Flothe, but he did spend a lot of time with Cindy Paulson learning about her side of the story, her life, and how it all affected her. She has done several interviews about her experience and has moved on with her life, but her encounter with Hansen changed her forever. She lives with the knowledge that he did not intend her to be one of his typical rape victims, free to go after enduring his nightmare. Cindy Paulson saved herself from becoming another red X on an aviation map behind a headboard, and that is something that she will never be able to forget or completely come to terms with. But she has used her story to help share her strength and her hardships.

Most people know about Hansen only because of the movie *The Frozen Ground*, but for many, that is enough to chill them to the bone. Hansen preyed upon people, women who he saw as less than himself. He was a man deranged, mentally ill, and with an uncontrollable need to feel powerful by diminishing other lives. He found pleasure in rape and death. He compared his victims to game, to wild animals. He saw these women, with their difficult and challenging but very human lives, as just another day in the woods.

"Nerve, nerve, nerve!" he panted, as he dashed along. A blue gap showed between the trees dead ahead. Ever nearer drew the hounds. Rainsford forced himself on toward that gap. He reached it. It was the shore of the sea. Across a cove he could see the gloomy gray stone of the chateau. Twenty feet below him the sea rumbled and hissed. Rainsford hesitated. He heard the hounds. Then he leaped far out into the sea... .

When the general and his pack reached the place by the sea, the Cossack stopped. For some minutes he stood regarding the blue-green expanse of water. He shrugged his shoulders. Then be sat down, took a drink of brandy from a silver flask, lit a cigarette, and hummed a bit from Madame Butterfly.

—"The Most Dangerous Game" by Richard Connell

Further Readings

BOOKS
Mindhunter by John Douglas

Hunted on Ice: The Search for Alaskan Serial Killer Robert Hansen by Reagan Martin

Butcher, Baker, the True Story of a Serial Killer Leland E. Hale and Walter Gilmour

FILM
Hidden City "Robert Hansen's Most Dangerous Game" (2012) Television Show

Hunter's Game (1999) Documentary

Ice Cold Killers "Hunting Humans" (2012) Television Show

Appendix: The Timeline

1939—February 15: Robert Christian Hansen is born to Christian and Edna Hansen in Esterville, Iowa.

1949—Hansen begins working for his father in the family bakery. He is dealing with stress brought on by a severe stutter and religiously fundamentalist, overbearing parents who force the left-handed boy to fit in by writing with his right hand.

1951—Stuttering, acne and the awkwardness of puberty decrease Hansen's ability to fit in socially, and he begins to deal with rage and inadequacy issues.

1953—Hansen enters high school. He does not have much of a social life but participates in multiple sports and after-school activities (basketball, pep club, chorus, track, long distance, and long/high jump). He still works in the bakery but has taken up hunting with guns and bows, as well as fishing, as a way to "get the anger out."

1957—Hansen graduates from high school.
—After signing up for the U.S. Army Reserve, he is flown out to basic training in Fort Dix in New Jersey.
—While stationed at Fort Knox, Kentucky, Hansen has his first sexual experience, with a prostitute.

1959—Hansen finishes his first year in the Army Reserve and is moved to "weekend warrior" status in which he trains one weekend a month and two weeks a year. He moves back home to live with his parents and work in the bakery. He also began volunteering at the police academy as a drill instructor.

1960—Hansen meets a young woman in town and marries her a short time later.
—December 7: Hansen decides to let out some of his anger about how he was treated in school. He recruits a teenager (possibly by force) to go with him to the county school bus garage, where they set the building on fire. He is sentenced to three years for the arson.
—December: Hansen's wife files for divorce.

1962—June: Hansen is released after serving 20 months of his sentence. Psychological evaluations state that he has child-like impulses and anger as well as issues with self-esteem and social interactions.

1963—Hansen meets Darla and marries her very shortly afterward.

1967—Robert and Darla Hansen move to Alaska to start over with a new life. Hansen steps up his hunting hobby, stalking bigger game in Alaska's large wilderness areas.

1969—Hansen submits a trophy animal to Pope & Young and garners an entry in the record books.

1970—Hansen secures a second entry into the trophy hunting record books.

1971—Hansen finds himself in the record books again for two more big game trophies.
—November: Hansen pulls a gun on a woman in traffic in Spenard and demands that she get into his car. She flees and Hansen is arrested, but he is immediately released on bail to await trial.

—Hansen is arrested again, this time for kidnapping, rape, and assault with a deadly weapon. The victim, an 18-year-old prostitute, fails to show up in court and the charges are dropped.
—December 23: 17-year-old Celia "Beth" Van Zanten goes missing from Anchorage, Alaska.
—December 25: Beth's body is found at McHugh State Park.

1972—Hansen stands trial for the weapons charge and is sentenced to five years in prison.
—March: Hansen begins serving his sentence and applies for parole.
—June: Hansen is granted parole and moves into a halfway house for psychiatric supervision and reform.
—December: Hansen is released from the halfway house.

1973—July 7: 17-year-old Megan Emerick goes missing in Anchorage.

1975—23-year-old Mary K. Thill goes missing from Seward.
—Hansen is accused of assault and rape by a prostitute who then stops cooperating with police. No charges are brought.

1976—Hansen is caught stealing a chainsaw from Fred Meyer's, a store in Anchorage. Due to his previous felony convictions for arson and weapons violations, he is sentenced to five years in prison.

1978—August: Hansen appeals to the parole board on the grounds that five years was an unduly harsh sentence for the theft of a chainsaw. He is granted parole but told to seek psychiatric treatment; however this condition is never enforced.
—Hansen applies for a pilot's license but is denied because he has a prescription for lithium. This causes him to discontinue the medication.

1980—June 28: 24-year-old Roxanne Easland goes missing in Anchorage.

—July 21: Near Eklutna Road, the badly decomposed body of a young woman later dubbed "Eklutna Annie" is found.

—July: Joanne Messina goes missing from Seward.

—September 6: 41-year-old Lisa Futrell goes missing in Anchorage.

—The body of Joanne Messina is found in a gravel pit near Eklutna Road.

1981—Hansen files a fraudulent claim with his insurance company stating that his house was burglarized and his valuable hunting trophies were stolen. He receives a sizable payout.

—Hansen uses the money from his insurance settlement to open his own bakery in a mini-mall in Anchorage. He becomes known in the community for his donuts and polite demeanor.

—November 17: 23-year-old Sherry Morrow goes missing from Anchorage.

—December 2: 22-year-old Andrea Altiery goes missing from Anchorage.

1982—Hansen purchases a Piper Super Club prop plane with the registration identifier N3089Z. He uses the plane to get to more secluded regions of the Alaskan wilderness for his legitimate hunting trips. He also uses it, initially, to dump bodies in more rural areas; toward the end of his killing spree he will fly his victims to the desolate forests to "hunt" them.

—May 26: 23-year-old Sue Luna goes missing in Anchorage.

—September 12: While on a hunting trip, an off-duty police officer and some friends find the body of Sherry Morrow along the bank of the Knik River.

1983—April 25: 31-year-old Paula Goulding goes missing from Anchorage.

—June 13: Cindy Paulson is kidnapped, raped, and tortured by Hansen. She escapes and goes to police. Hansen is investigated, but charges are dropped because he is able to provide an alibi.

During the investigation, police search his home, car, and plane, finding information that will later prove valuable.

—September 2: Paula Goulding's body is found in a shallow grave near where Sherry Morrow's body was located, confirming to the Alaska State Troopers that they have a serial killer. The FBI is called in to assist with the case. Detective Glenn Flothe uncovers Hansen's incriminating past, and criminal psychologist John Douglas creates a profile of the serial killer.

—October 27: Hansen is brought in for questioning while his plane and house are searched. Authorities find the gun used in the murders, a map marked with red X's indicating the location of bodies, and IDs and jewelry from victims.

—November 3: A grand jury indicts Hansen on charges of first degree assault on a person, second degree theft, insurance fraud, and five counts of misconduct with a deadly weapon.

—November 20: The crime lab finishes its ballistics analysis of the bullets found in the victims and Hansen's .223 Mini-14 rifle and announces a match.

1984—February 18: Hansen enters a plea of guilty in the murders of Paula Goulding, Sherry Monroe, Joanna Messina, and the unidentified body known as Eklutna Annie.

—February 22: Hansen's defense attorney, Fred Dewey, and District Attorney Victor Krumm make a deal that in exchange for his full confession in the four murders for which he has been indicted, Hansen will not be prosecuted for the other killings and will serve his time in a federal prison. Hansen accepts the deal.

—February 27: Hansen is given the maximum sentence of 461 years plus life without the possibility of parole. He is sent to the Lewisburg Federal Penitentiary in Pennsylvania.

—April 24: The body of Sue Luna is found along the Knik River.

—April 24: Malai Larsen's body is found in a parking lot by the Old Knik Bridge at the Knik River.

—April 25: DeLynn Frey's body is found by Horseshoe Lake.

—April 26: Teresa Watson's body is found on the Kenai Peninsula.

—April 26: Angela Feddern's body is found near Figure Eight Lake.

—April 29: Tamara Pederson's body is found a mile and a half from the Old Knik Bridge along the Knik River.
—May 9: Lisa Futrell's body is found south of the Old Knik Bridge by the Knik River.

1988—Hansen is transferred to the Spring Creek Correctional Center in Seward, Alaska, as one of the first inmates in the new prison.

1990—Darla Hansen files for divorce and leaves Alaska because of the harassment and embarrassment. She and her children flee to Arkansas to try to start over.

1995—John Douglas publishes his book *Mindhunter*, which contains details about his part in the investigation of Hansen and the Alaskan serial killings.

1999- An episode of *The FBI Files*, "Hunter's Game," airs about Hansen.

2003—February 21: Police use true crime television shows and other media channels to try to identify Eklutna Annie and the other unknown victims from the jewelry found in Hansen's home.

2007—*Crime Stories* airs an episode documenting the case of the "Butcher Baker."

2010—May 12: An episode of *Criminal Minds*, "Exit Wounds," discusses Hansen.

2012—January 25: *Alaska: Ice Cold Killers* on Investigation Discovery documents the Hansen case with an episode titled "Hunting Humans."
—February 21: The Travel Channel's *Hidden City* episode "Anchorage: Robert Hansen's Most Dangerous Game, the Legend of Blackjack Sturges, Eskimo Hu" airs.

—February 22: The *Law and Order: Special Victims Unit* episode "Hunting Ground" depicts a fictional rendition of Hansen.

2013—The movie *The Frozen Ground* is released. Starring John Cusack as Robert Hansen, Nicholas Cage as Detective Glenn Flothe, and Vanessa Hudgens as Cindy Paulson, it portrays the case from the perspective of Cindy and Detective Flothe.

2014—August 21: Robert Hansen dies in a prison hospital in Alaska at the age of 75.

Also by Jack Smith

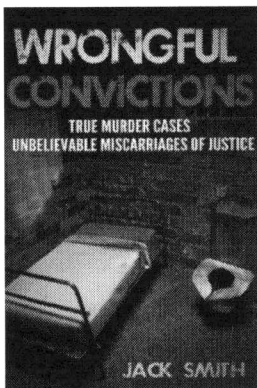

THE HAPPY FACE
MURDERER
The Life of Serial Killer Keith Hunter Jesperson
Jack Smith

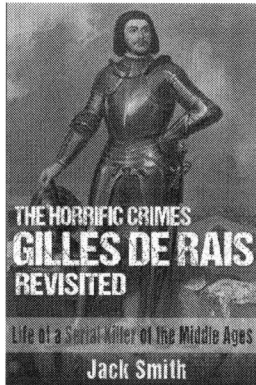

THE HORRIFIC CRIMES
GILLES DE RAIS
REVISITED
Life of a Serial Killer of The Middle Ages
Jack Smith

THE BEAST OF
BIRKENSHAW
LIFE OF SERIAL KILLER
PETER MANUEL
JACK SMITH

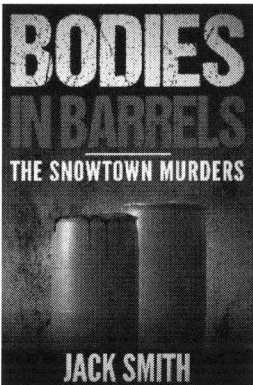

BODIES
IN BARRELS
THE SNOWTOWN MURDERS
JACK SMITH

HIDDEN
BRUTALITY
LIFE OF SERIAL KILLER CARL EUGENE WATTS
JACK SMITH

THE SPOKANE
KILLER
The Life of Serial Killer Robert Lee Yates Jr
Jack Smith

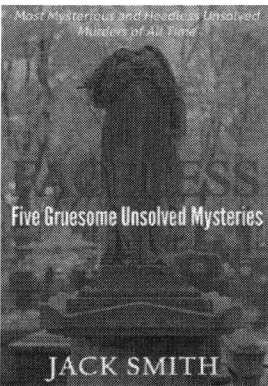

Most Mysterious and Headless Unsolved Murders of All Time
HEADLESS
Five Gruesome Unsolved Mysteries
JACK SMITH

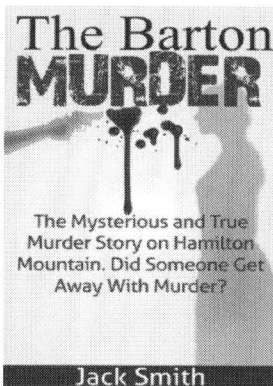

The Barton
MURDER
The Mysterious and True
Murder Story on Hamilton
Mountain. Did Someone Get
Away With Murder?
Jack Smith

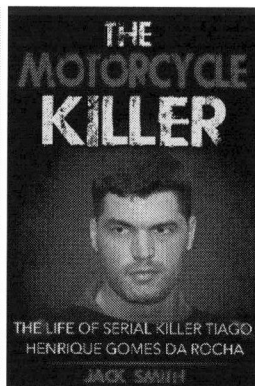

THE
MOTORCYCLE
KILLER
THE LIFE OF SERIAL KILLER TIAGO
HENRIQUE GOMES DA ROCHA
JACK SMITH

THE CROSS COUNTRY KILLER
Life of Serial Killer Tommy Lynn Sells
Jack Smith

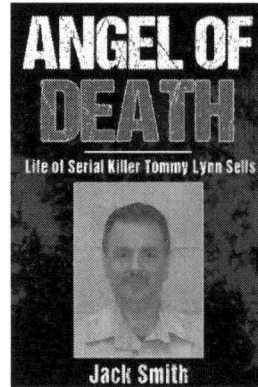

ANGEL OF DEATH
Life of Serial Killer Tommy Lynn Sells
Jack Smith

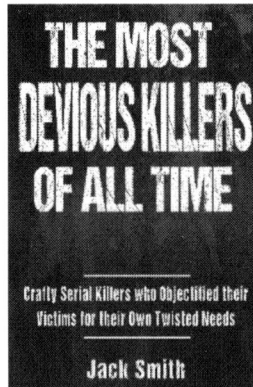

THE MOST DEVIOUS KILLERS OF ALL TIME
Crafty Serial Killers who Objectified their Victims for their Own Twisted Needs
Jack Smith

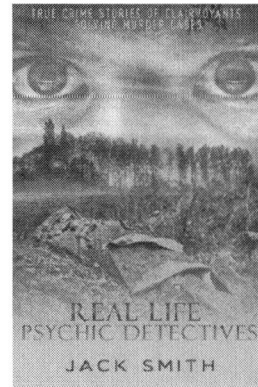

REAL LIFE PSYCHIC DETECTIVES
JACK SMITH

References

Andrews, Laurel. "'Frozen Ground' serial killer Hansen dead." Alaska Dispatch News. August 21, 2014. Accessed August 15, 2017. https://www.adn.com/crime-justice/article/infamous-alaska-serial-killer-robert-hansen-dies/2014/08/21/.

"Antisocial Personality Disorder." Psychology Today. April 19, 2017. Accessed August 19, 2017. https://www.psychologytoday.com/conditions/antisocial-personality-disorder.

"Bipolar Affective Disorder (Manic Depression)." MyVMC. September 30, 2015. Accessed August 19, 2017. https://www.myvmc.com/diseases/bipolar-affective-disorder-manic-depression/.

Blanco, Juan Ignacio. "Robert Hansen." Murderpedia, the encyclopedia of murderers. Accessed August 15, 2017. http://murderpedia.org/male.H/h/hansen-robert.htm.

Bonnie. "Serial Killer: *Butcher Baker* Robert Hansen." My Life of Crime. August 24, 2014. Accessed August 15, 2017. https://mylifeofcrime.wordpress.com/2014/08/23/serial-killer-butcher-baker-robert-hansen-killed-at-least-17-women-sentenced-to-years-in-prison-died-8212014/.

Brennan, Tom. Murder at 40 below: true crime stories from Alaska. Kenmore, WA: Epicenter Press, 2001.

Connell, Richard. "The Most Dangerous Game." 1924.

Coppock, Michael. "Alaska's serial killer: Hunting strippers in the bush." Juneau Empire. April 11, 2008. Accessed August 15, 2017. http://juneauempire.com/stories/041108/nei_267504580.shtml#.WZNgUXG1vDc.

"Denied by Hansen, Pt. 1: Megan Emerick." Butcher, Baker. January 12, 2017. Accessed August 19, 2017. http://butcherbaker.net/wordpress/denied-by-hansen-pt-1-megan-emerick/.

Douglas, John E., and Mark Olshaker. Mindhunter: Inside the FBI's Elite Serial Crime Unit. New York: Pocket books, 1996.

DuClos, Bernard. (1993). Fair game. NY: St. Martin's. (ISBN 0-312-92905-6)

Dunham, Mike. "Grisly legacy of 'Eklutna Annie'." Alaska Dispatch News. September 29, 2016. Accessed August 19, 2017. https://www.adn.com/alaska-news/article/grisly-legacy-eklutna-annie/2012/07/15/.

Etherealairhead, ~. "Ode to Doe: Horseshoe Harriet." A Kitten's Curiosity. February 26, 2017. Accessed August 19, 2017. https://etherealairhead.wordpress.com/2017/02/26/ode-to-doe-horseshoe-harriet/.

Ferri, Jessica. "Robert Hansen: The Alaskan Serial Killer Who Hunted Human Game." The Line Up. December 09, 2016. Accessed August 15, 2017. https://the-line-up.com/robert-hansen-the-serial-killer-who-hunted-human-game.

Gilmour, Walter & Hale, Leland E. (1991). *Butcher, baker: A true account of a serial murderer.* NY: Onyx Press. (ISBN 0-451-40276-6)

Good, Meaghan Elizabeth. "The Charley Project." The Charley Project. Accessed August 19, 2017. http://www.charleyproject.org/.

H, Reva. Sue Luna. July 18, 2000. Accessed August 19, 2017. http://www.murdervictims.com/voices/sue_luna.htm.

Hale, Leland E. "Unsolved Murder: Did Alaskan Serial Killer Robert Hansen Kill Beth van Zanten?" The Line Up. July 19, 2017. Accessed August 19, 2017. https://the-line-up.com/unsolved-murder-did-alaskan-serial-killer-robert-hansen-kill-beth-van-zanten.

"Hansen v. State." Justia Law. Accessed August 19, 2017. http://law.justia.com/cases/alaska/supreme-court/1978/3412-1.html.

"If film makes Hansen's victims real, the story's worth retelling." Alaska Dispatch News. April 28, 2016. Accessed August 19, 2017. https://www.adn.com/voices/article/if-film-makes-hansens-victims-real-storys-worth-retelling/2011/08/01/.

Krajicek, David J. "Serial killer's sick 'revenge' in the Alaskan frontier." NY Daily News. August 31, 2014. Accessed August 15, 2017. http://www.nydailynews.com/news/crime/serial-killer-sick-revenge-alaskan-frontier-article-1.1922167.

Lundberg, Murray. "Robert Hansen A Serial Killer in Alaska." ExploreNorth.com—Your Gateway to the North. February 11, 2000. Accessed August 15, 2017. http://www.explorenorth.com/library/crime/alaska_serial_killer.html.

McLaughlin, Emily, Megan Donnelly, Carrie Draper, and Jennifer Duncan. PDF. Radford, VA: Department of Psychology Radford University. https://www.google.com/url?sa=t&rct=j&q=&esrc=s&source=web&cd=12&cad=rja&uact=8&ved=0ahUKEwjRqpaIjNrVAhWE4iYKHZpGD3c4ChAWCCwwAQ&url=http%3A%2F%2Fmaamodt.asp.radford.edu%2FPsyc%2520405%2Fserial%2520killers%2FHansen%2C%2520Robert%2520-%2520fall%2C%25202005.pdf&usg=AFQjCNEemgH1T4oty4qguzFo1I3_3lGDwQ

"Missing girl tips revive Alaska cold case." UPI. September 28, 2008. Accessed August 19, 2017. http://www.upi.com/Missing-girl-tips-revive-Alaska-cold-case/15701222624602/.

"Never Forget Me." Facebook . 2014. Accessed August 19, 2017. https://www.facebook.com/pg/WeWontForgetThem/photos/?tab=album&album_id=922946237719414. Eklutna Annie Images

Olshaker, Mark. "Robert Hansen: Good Riddance." Mindhunters. August 25, 2014. Accessed August 15, 2017. http://mindhuntersinc.com/robert-hansen-good-riddance/.

"Photos." Butcher, Baker, the True Story of a Serial Killer: Photos. Accessed August 15, 2017. http://butcherbaker.net/photos.html.

"Robert Hansen Archives Map." Butcher, Baker. November 8, 2013. Accessed August 19, 2017. http://butcherbaker.net/wordpress/tag/robert-hansen/.

Roberts, Sheila. "Director Scott Walker Talks THE FROZEN GROUND, His Feature Directorial Debut, and Upcoming Werewolf Comedy BULLET BLOOD WILD." Collider. February 09, 2015. Accessed August 19, 2017. http://collider.com/scott-walker-frozen-ground-interview/.

"Serial Killers: Nature vs. Nurture." National Center of Crisis Management. Accessed August 19, 2017. http://www.nc-cm.org/article213.htm.

"Sue Luna remembered." Sue Luna remembered—Democratic Underground. May 16, 2008. Accessed August 23, 2017. https://www.democraticunderground.com/discuss/duboard.php?az=view_all&address=341x12804.

Townsend, Catherine, and Mike McFadden. "Serial Killer And "Butcher Baker" Robert Hansen Hunted Women Down In The Woods." CrimeFeed. February 15, 2017. Accessed August 15, 2017. http://crimefeed.com/2017/02/crime-history-robert-hansen-who-hunted-women-in-alaska/.

Upthegrove, Rachel, Christine Chard, Lisa Jones, Katherine Gordon-Smith, Liz Forty, Ian Jones, and Nick Craddock. "Adverse childhood events and psychosis in bipolar affective disorder." *The British Journal of Psychiatry*. March 01, 2015. Accessed August 19, 2017. http://bjp.rcpsych.org/content/206/3/191.

"Watching True Crime Stories." Tapatalk-powered-by. May 3, 2008. Accessed August 15, 2017. https://www.tapatalk.com/groups/watchingrobertpickton88015/robert-hansen-alaskan-serial-killer-t1557.html.

Printed in Great Britain
by Amazon